'LOVE IS HIS MEANING'

'LOVE IS HIS MEANING'

THE IMPACT OF JULIAN OF NORWICH

JOHN SKINNER

GRACEWING

First published in 2013 by
Gracewing
2 Southern Avenue
Leominster
Herefordshire HR6 0QF
United Kingdom
www.gracewing.co.uk

ISBN 978 085244 818 2

Typeset by Gracewing

Cover design by Bernardita Peña Hurtado

For Judith, my family and friends all

CONTENTS

INTRODUCTION

I have read both Teresa of Avila and John of the Cross as well as a library of spiritual works; I have conversed over the years with the Carthusians, prayed and worked in their community, but not one can speak more directly of prayer and intimacy with our Maker, indeed of his loving intimacy with us, than Julian of Norwich, our greatest spiritual teacher. I first met this remarkable lady sixty years ago when I was a young Jesuit novice. A small red pamphlet came to hand. It contained brief quotations from Julian's *Revelation of Love* arranged as points for meditation. I was at once excited by her vivid and inviting sayings:

> God is nearer to us than our own soul ... the goodness of God is our highest prayer and it comes down to us to meet our very least need ... for just as the body is clad in clothes and the flesh in skin and the bones in flesh with the heart in the breast, so are we, soul and body, clothed and wrapped around in the goodness of God.

A uniquely ravishing voice speaking out loud and clear from the Fourteenth Century. I went straight to my Master of Novices asking who is this woman? Without a word, Father Walkerley—'The George', as we called him—crossed to his bookshelves, trailed his finger along the top shelf and retrieved the 1901 edition, the seminal translation by Grace Warrack. In spite of her favouring archaic English—'it passeth ... thou comest'—a mannerism that lasted into the twentieth century with James Walsh's Orchard Edition, I was utterly taken by her approach to the spiritual life. But such enthusiasm did not last. Like many another coming to Julian for the first time, I soon became lost in her maze of circular narrative.

It was only many years later, when I was privileged to publish my own modern translation, using inclusive language while still retaining the rhythmic lilt of Julian's Middle English, that I began to penetrate her deeper meaning and her motives for writing the very first book to be composed by a woman in the English tongue. The difficulty in tackling Julian's book is that it is not a book at all. That is to say, she composed her Long Text (there is also a shorter version to be found in the British Library) over a period of some twenty years, adding and expanding, editing and correcting. And although her text follows an exposition of each of her Sixteen Revelations, her account of them is continually confounded by complex circular reasoning. Julian is every inch a woman: she ponders and repeats, returns again and again to the main themes of the mysteries which have been revealed to her, reworking them with fresh insights.

The end result of such complexities, I believe, is that most readers coming to her text for the first time are soon defeated. They cannot see the beauty of the wood as a whole since they continually bump up against tree after tree. It might not be too much of an exaggeration to suggest that all most people can tell of Julian is Eliot's much plagiarized 'all shall be well, and all shall be well...' But Julian's treasure store is so much richer than this simple and frequently misplaced saw. For she speaks eloquently of every Christian's daily duty: to welcome the loving intimacy of our Maker and to express this amazing gift by sharing it throughout the human family.

> There will be gifts for you: a full measure, pressed down, shaken together, and running over, will be poured into your lap. (Lk 6:38)

It is my belief that Julian could have done with a skilful and courageous copy editor of the kind they hire in American publishing houses. But in Fourteenth Century Norwich, no such person was even thought of. The aim of this book, then, is to present my readers with a generous selection of key passages, using my own translation, but setting them out so as to shed more light—and hopefully order—on Julian's tangled exposition. And if I succeed, if only in part, I feel confident that my beloved author will forgive such radical treatment of her sacred text.

So what do we know of Julian, apart from her two texts? Her life story is simply told in her own words, but she leaves much unsaid. On the eighth day of May, 1373, at the age of 32, she was struck down by a sudden sickness which seemed to herself and those who came to her aid as life threatening. She slowly lost control of her limbs and could do little more than stare fixedly at the crucifix which her priest had brought as he anointed her with the Last Rites. She lay like this for the inside of a week and during this time she experienced a series of visions or 'showings' numbering sixteen in all. She did not die but lived on for several decades into old age. We are not told of her status at this critical moment in her life, but we do know that subsequently she spent the remainder of her days as an anchorite living in her cell attached to the walls of the humble church of St Julian in the wool enriched city of Norwich.

Although Julian is keen to tell us all about her interior life and the impact of her revelations, she tells us nothing of her background or previous circumstances. We have no name for her, save that of the dedication of her Norwich church. Her two roomed cell, where she and a servant spent their days, survived well into the twentieth century when, finally, it was badly damaged by enemy bombing in the Second World War. The church has since been repaired and a small side chapel is dedicated to our holy woman, while nearby there is a purpose built Julian Centre with library and information facilities catering for the growing number of pilgrims drawn to her shrine.

In spite of the paucity of biographical details, we still have several important historical pointers. We know for instance that she was visited by that peripatetic pilgrim, Margery Kempe; for that talkative lady tells us so in her book that she dictated. She appears to have sought counsel from Julian as to the authenticity of her own mystical experiences and she tells us that the two women spent some days together. Julian's advice was simple and wise:

> When she (Julian) heard about our Lord's wonderful goodness, the anchoress thanked him with all her heart for visiting me (Margery) like this. Her advice was that I should remain always obedient to God's will, carrying out with all my strength whatever prompting he put into my soul. But I must be careful that these were not contrary to God's glory or to the benefit of my fellow Christians. Because, if this were the case, then such promptings were not those of a good spirit, but rather of an evil spirit. The Holy Spirit can never urge us to do anything against charity; for if he did so, he would be acting against his own self, for he is the sum of charity.[1]

It is useless lamenting our lack of biographical knowledge of Julian for her very own writings offer us an intimate insight into the mind and heart of this great lady. One has to go back 1500 years to Augustine himself to find an equally open account of an emerging soul. But not even one of the Greatest Doctors of the Church in his *Confessions*

1   Margery Kempe, *The Book of Margery Kempe,*translated by John Skinner, chapter 17.

is quite the match of Julian as she slowly comes to fathom 'the meaning' of Christ revealing to her his love for his human family in these Sixteen Showings.

Let us then turn to Julian for her own simple account of her momentous experience lasting over a single week.

CHAPTER I

God's Son fell with Adam into the valley of the Maiden's womb, she who was fairest daughter of Adam, in order to excuse Adam from all his blame in heaven and in earth; then mightily he fetched him out of hell.

These Revelations were showed to a simple creature that could not letter in the year of Our Lord 1373, on the eighth day of May. Which creature had first desired three gifts from God. The first was mind of his passion; the second was a bodily sickness in her youth at thirty years of age; and the third was to have of God three wounds.

Julian is precise in her account of what happened to her, also as to her state of mind. She gives no personal details save to disclose her inner disposition. As she carefully explains:

The first [desire] was mind of his passion...although I believed I already had some feeling for Christ's passion, yet I desired more by the grace of God. I thought at that time to be like Mary Magdalene and others who were Christ's lovers, and therefore I desired a bodily sight wherein I might have more knowledge of the bodily pains of our Saviour, and of the compassion of our Lady and all his true lovers that saw his pains in that time; for I would be one of them and suffer with him.

Seven of her sixteen showings relate directly to Christ's passion on the cross; and her prayer to become one of the few who did not abandon him in his last hours was truly answered. She witnesses his passion close to and her descriptions are vivid in the extreme. Some readers recoil from these passages, finding them too explicit and lacking in taste. But unless we accept the reality of Christ's passion and crucifixion, we risk missing the central meaning of God's loving relationship with his creation. For it is precisely this *kenosis*—God's self-emptying—his act of Creation in the first place, his willingness 'to become lower than the Angels' by his Incarnation, the Word-Act made Flesh, followed by his embracing the most shaming death possible, and, finally, his dying scream of abandonment upon the cross, that we may begin to measure the infinite nature of his Love for his human family.

But before we deal in detail with Julian's extraordinary revelations, I wish to start at the very centre of her work. Her book comprises eighty six chapters, each of them comparatively short—two to three pages. But midway comes chapter 51; and it is curiously out of context with the remainder of her text. Firstly, it runs to twelve pages; and again its material seems out of step with all that has gone before. And yet as it unfolds, we are presented with a brilliant tableau that offers a dramatic enactment of the purpose and economy of the Incarnation. It was Anselm who pondered *Cur Deus homo?* Why *did* God become a man like us: Julian answers Anselm in masterly fashion.

Julian's chief stumbling block is sin. Simply put: sin is a fact, but what exactly is it. Her answer comes: it is 'no thing'. Yet such an answer slips through her hands; for clearly the consequences of sin are paramount. Sin is the very scourge of all Creation, the cancer for all to experience. This conundrum arises because Christ has cured sin. Although we still languish in Adam's sinful state, Christ beckons us forward.

'God is not wroth... I saw no wrath in God.'

At this point, Julian is utterly lost. She can proceed no further in her narrative. Until, as she discloses in chapter 51, she is shown a parable of a lord and a servant. Mysterious at first, as Julian seeks out every last detail, its rich meaning unfolds. This is none other than a wonderful parable of Christ's working mankind's salvation: his Again-Making 'in every soul that shall be saved'.

And then our courteous Lord answered by showing, none too clearly, a wonderful example of a lord who has a servant; and he enlightened my understanding as to them both.

I was shown two persons in bodily likeness, namely a lord and a servant; and at the same time God gave me spiritual understanding. The lord sits solemnly in rest and in peace, while the servant stands by, reverently before his lord, ready to do his lord's will. The lord looks upon his servant with very sweet and loving gaze, and then meekly sends him to a certain place to do his will. The servant not only goes, but he starts out suddenly and runs with great haste for the love he has to do his lord's will. And straightway he falls into a boggy dell and takes very great hurt. And then he groans and moans and wails and writhes, but neither can he rise up nor may he help himself in any way. And in all this, the most mischief that I saw for him was his lack of comfort; for he could not turn his face and look toward his loving lord, who, still very close to him, was his only comfort.

The key phrase here is 'none too clearly', for there is much work to be done before Julian discerns the full 'meaning' of this quaint parable or play. As a young girl living in Norwich, Julian would have rejoiced with all the other children as they followed the annual Mystery Plays trundling through the cobbled streets. The Guilds each had their own story to tell: from Adam and Eve to the Harrowing of Hell. And great was the competition to decorate each cart more dramatically and lavishly than the next.

Julian's dreamlike parable seems to be her own private Mystery Play that she must now work to unravel.

He enlightened my understanding as to them both [the lord and his servant]. This sight was shown doubly in regard of the lord; and it was shown doubly in regard of the servant. The first part was shown spiritually with bodily likeness, and the other was shown more spiritually without any image.

By replaying her parable, Julian slowly unravels its every detail to discover the deeper meaning of what she has been shown. First comes her vivid tableau 'shown spiritually with bodily likeness'; then, over 'twenty years and three months', comes her full realisation of its inner meaning. The twofold role of both lord and servant become transparent. To begin with the servant is stuck in his 'boggy dell', and yet Julian sees that the lord, far from blaming him for his carelessness, 'continues to behold him with the same tenderness and love'.

Then the courteous lord speaks his mind: 'Lo, lo, my beloved servant, what harm and disease he has taken in the service he undertook for my love, yes, and with such good will! Is it not right that I reward him for his terror and his fright, his hurt and all his woe? And not only this, does it not fall to me to give him a gift that would be better and more reward to him than ever he had before? Or else it seems I give him no thanks at all.'

As suddenly as her parable appeared, so too it vanishes. But Julian knows how important is its meaning. She tells us of her fascination at the parable and her certainty that it holds a vital answer to her own predicament as regards sin and God's ever present love. She too is stuck in her own 'boggy dell'. But she must works things through:

For in the servant that was shown for Adam, as I will say, were many different properties that simply could not all belong solely to Adam on his own. And so, at this time, I was very confused, and the full understanding of this marvellous parable was not given to me then. Notwithstanding, I saw and understood that every revelation contains much that is still hidden. I have the means whereby I ought to believe and trust in our Lord God that of the same goodness by which he showed it, and for the same end, right so of the same goodness and for the same end, he will declare it to us when it is his will.

For twenty years less three months after the time of showing, I had teaching inwardly, as I shall tell: 'It is your task to take heed of all the properties and conditions that were shown in the parable, though you think they are mysterious and hard to see.. I assented willingly and with great desire ... Beginning with my beholding the lord and his servant, and the place where he sat, the colour of his clothing...

'For twenty years less three months...' might suggest that this mysterious parable which is to shed so much light on Julian's journey belongs to the sixteen showings and is contemporaneous with them. But I believe otherwise. For one thing, their narration fits, almost like a hinge or coda, midway in our text. Moreover, once unravelled Julian's pace picks up and her mood changes. Gone is the puzzle-

ment over the nature of sin and God's seeming indifference
to mankind's waywardness ('I saw no wrath in God...');
instead, Julian becomes quite lyrical as she describes the
intimate working of the Trinity in the human soul before
she unfolds her sixteenth and final revelation. My own
suggestion, therefore, is that the parable belongs as a
codicil to the revelations, presenting a fresh and original
insight into the mystery of the Incarnation and Christ's
saving work for his human family.

The vision of the tableau is one thing: its rich meaning
will only become apparent by attending to each and every
detail it contains. Like some vivid dream imprinted in her
mind, Julian replays its memory, savouring every least
detail. And she ponders these with superbly flowing
descriptions: remember, this woman, a contemporary of
Chaucer, is the first female tongue to announce our newly
forming English language. Middle English is the spring-
board for Shakespeare and all that is to follow.

And so began the teaching which I had at that time...

The place where the lord sat was simple; he sat upon
the barren earth, in a desert, alone in a wilderness, his
clothing was wide and flowing, very seemly as befits
a lord; the colour of his clothing was blue as azure most
solemn and fair. His mien was merciful, his face was
bronzed, of feature fair; his eyes were dark and lus-
trous and showed a loving pity: his watchful gaze
extended far and wide, seeming to fill the endless
heavens. And with this lovely look he watched his
servant continually, especially as he saw his falling; I
thought to myself it might melt our hearts for love and
break them in two for joy. This kindly looking showed
a beautiful intermingling that was marvellous to
behold: on the one part it was compassion and pity,
for the other joy and bliss. This joy and bliss so far

surpasses the compassion and pity as heaven is above earth: for the pity was earthly and the bliss was of heaven. The compassion in the pity of the Father was for the falling of Adam, who is his most loved creature: the joy and the bliss belonged to his beloved Son who is always with the Father. His loving and merciful gaze filled the whole earth, even descending down to hell with Adam, and by this continual pity Adam was kept from everlasting death.

Swept up in this fast moving narrative, we need to pause and remember its context. Julian has spent long hours, day by day, pondering her curious play scene. And now she begins to perceive its inner meaning that might answer her longing, how *does* God not merely tolerate, but 'blissfully' love his creation in fallen Adam, that is humankind. For 'with this lovely look he watched his servant continually, especially as he saw his falling': 'the pity was earthly and the bliss was of heaven'. With deft brush strokes of her prayerful imaging, Julian is conjuring a masterful theology of our salvation. Christ has taken human flesh, that is Adam's soiled smock to bring it before his Father and do his will of service.

And this same mercy and pity dwells with humankind until such time as we come up into heaven. But in this life we are blinded, and therefore we may not see the Father, our God, as he is. And whenever of his goodness he wishes to show himself to us, he does so familiarly—as man.

Notwithstanding, I saw very clearly we should learn and come to know that the Father is not man. But his sitting on the barren earth in that desert has this meaning: he made the human soul to be his city, his own dwelling place, for it is to him the most pleasing of all his works. But since the time that Adam fell into sorrow and pain, he was not fit to serve that noble office; and yet our kind Father would prepare no other place, but he sits upon the earth abiding with mankind that is earthbound, until such time as his beloved Son by his grace has bought again his city into noble fairness by his hard travail.

After years of prayerful meditation, Julian begins to fathom the full significance. Her lyrical prose in this wonderful passage reveals her mounting excitement.

And yet I marvelled as I continued to behold the lord and this same servant in more detail. For I saw the lord sitting solemnly and the servant standing reverently before his lord. And in the servant there is a double understanding: one without, another within.

Outwardly he was simply clad, like a labourer ready for work; and he stood very near his lord, though not directly in front but rather to one side, on the left. His clothing was a white smock, unpleated, old and fast-stained, dyed with the sweat of his body; strait it fitted him, falling short about a handspan below the knee, threadbare too, seeming that soon it would be quite worn through, and ready to be ragged and rent. And at this I marvelled greatly, thinking to myself: 'Surely this is not the sort of clothing for a servant who is so loved to wear as he stands before his great lord.'

Yet inwardly I saw, within him, a ground of love, such a love he bore toward the lord that was even like the love his lord bore toward him.

Here we have the first hint of the inner life of the Trinity— Father loving his Son, the Son reflecting that same Love back to his Father—which, 'by mercy and grace', will be offered to his human family by 'the working' of the Servant.

The servant, in his wisdom, saw inwardly that there was only one thing to be done that would prove honourable service for his lord. Then the servant, of his love, not for his own reward nor of any gain to himself, started off in haste and ran at the bidding of his lord to perform the one task which was his will and worship.

Outwardly, it seemed as if he had been a labourer continuously over a long time; yet by the inward sight I had, both of the lord and his servant, it seemed he was fresh, that is to say, newly begun to work, a servant never before sent out.

Now there was a treasure in the earth which the lord loved. I marvelled and thought what it could be. And I was answered in my understanding: 'It is a meat most desirable that will please the lord.'

For I saw the lord sitting like a man, and I saw neither meat nor drink that one might serve him; that was one strangeness. Another was that this same solemn lord had no other servant than the one he had sent out. I considered this carefully, thinking what kind of labour it might be that the servant would do. And then I understood that he would do the greatest labour and the hardest work—that is, he would be a gardener, delving and diking, toiling and sweating to turn the earth over and trench it; and he would water the plants in their time.

And he would continue in all this work and make sweet water flow and noble fruits aplenty to spring forth; and these he would bring before his lord and serve them to him to please him. And he would never return again until he had prepared this meat all ready,

just as he knew was to his lord's liking. And then he
would take this meat, and drink too, and lay it worshipfully before his lord.

All this time, the lord would be sitting in the same
place awaiting his servant whom he had sent out. And
still I wondered from where the servant came; for I
saw in the lord that he had within himself endless life
and all manner of goodness, save only that treasure
that was in the earth—yet this itself was grounded in
the lord in a marvellous deep vein of endless love—but
it was not completely acceptable until this same
servant prepared it so nobly and set it all before him,
presenting it of his own accord.

Apart from the lord there was nothing all around
but wilderness; and so I could not understand at all
what this example might mean, and still I continued
to puzzle whence the servant had come.

At this point, Julian realises the inner meaning of the
servant, who is two in one, the old Adam representing
fallen humankind, and the Son who, 'newly begun to work',
is poised to raise us up to stand at his side. Moreover, she
sees plainly that the Lord, his Father, is complicit in his
work. For it is the Father who sends his Son to 'be a
gardener, delving and diking, toiling and sweating' to
prepare 'the meat all ready, just as he knew was to his lord's
liking'.

Now in the servant is comprehended the Second
Person of the Trinity; and in the servant is comprehended Adam, that is to say all humankind. And
therefore when I say 'the Son', it means the Godhead
which is equal to the Father, and when I say 'the
servant', it means Christ's manhood which is the true
Adam. By the nearness of the servant the Son is

understood, and by the standing to the left side is understood Adam.

The lord is the Father, God. The servant is the Son, Christ Jesus. The Holy Spirit is equal love who is in them both.

When Adam fell, God's Son fell. For because of the faithful oneing which was made in heaven, God's son might not part from Adam—and in Adam is understood all humankind.

Adam fell from life into death, into the vale of this wretched world and after that into hell.

God's Son fell with Adam into the valley of the Maiden's womb, she who was the fairest daughter of Adam, in order to excuse Adam from all his blame in heaven and in earth.

Then mightily he fetched him out of hell!

By the wisdom and goodness of the servant is to be understood God's Son. By the poor labourer's clothing and his standing near the left side is understood the manhood of Adam, with all the mischief and feebleness that resulted; for in all this, our good Lord showed his own Son and Adam as but one man.

The virtue and the goodness that we have is of Jesus Christ, the feebleness and blindness is of Adam; both of which were shown in the servant. And so has our good Lord Jesus taken upon himself all our blame; and therefore our Father may assign, neither will he, no more blame to us than to his own Son, dearworthy Christ. Thus he was the servant even before his coming into the earth, who stood ready before the Father prepared against the time when he would send him to do that worshipful deed by which mankind would be brought once more into heaven; that is to say, notwithstanding that he is God, equal with the Father as

regards the Godhead, he already foresaw his purpose
to become man so as to save humankind in fulfilment
of his Father's will. So that he stood before his Father
as a servant, willingly taking upon himself all our debts.

And then he set off promptly in answer to his
Father's will, and at once he fell down low into the
Maiden's womb, regardless of himself or his hard
pains.

The white smock is his flesh; its plainness, that there
is nothing between the Godhead and the manhood; its
straitness, his poverty; its age comes from Adam's
wearing; the staining with sweat from Adam's labours;
while its shortness shows how the servant must labour.

And so I saw the Son standing, and he spoke his
purpose thus: 'Lo, my dear Father, I stand before you
in Adam's smock all ready to start and run my course.
I wish to be in the earth to do your service whenever
it is your will to send me. How long must I wait?'

Full well the Son knew when it was the Father's will
and how long he would wait; that is to say with respect
to the Godhead, for he is the Wisdom of the Father. So
that this meaning was shown of the manhood of
Christ; for all those that shall be saved by the sweet
Incarnation and blissful passion of Christ, they are all
of the manhood of Christ: for he is the head and we
are his members. Now to those members the day and
the time is not known when every passing woe and
sorrow shall come to an end and their everlasting joy
and bliss shall be fulfilled. Yet all the company of
heaven long to see that day and its time…

Now that the meaning is becoming clear, there seems no
end to the expressive beauty of her parable. Paul enunciates
the polarity between Adam and Christ in his first letter to
the Corinthians: 'Death came through one man and in the

same way the resurrection of the dead has come through one man. Just as all men die in Adam, so all men will be brought to life in Christ...If the soul has its own embodiment, so does the spirit have its own embodiment. The first *man*, Adam, as scripture says *became a living soul;* but the last Adam has become a life-giving spirit.' [1 Corinthians 15] Julian sees the servant labouring to prepare 'meat and drink to lay it worshipfully before his lord', a labour which we too must endure. And Paul concludes his chapter in similar fashion: 'Never give in then, my dear brothers, never admit defeat; keep on working at the Lord's work always, know that, in the Lord, you cannot be labouring in vain.'

Also in this marvellous parable, I have teaching set before me, just like the beginning of an ABC, whereby I may have some understanding of our Lord's meaning. For all that is hidden about this revelation is contained therein, notwithstanding all the revelations are full of secrets.

Julian is now spelling out her puzzle, just like the final clues of a crossword falling into place.

The sitting of the Father is token of his Godhead, that is to say, it shows rest and peace; for in the Godhead there may be no labour. And he showed himself as lord in token of our humanity. The standing of the servant betokens travail; being to one side and on the left is token of his unworthiness to stand an equal before his lord. His starting was the Godhead and his running was the manhood; for the Godhead starts from the Father into the Maiden's womb, falling into the taking of our kind; and in this falling he took great hurt; the hurt he took was the flesh in which he also had such feeling of deadly pains. In that he stood in dread before the lord, not straight in front of him, is token that his clothing was not honest to be standing straight in front of the lord. Nor could that, nor should that be his place while he was still a servant; neither might he sit at rest and peace with the lord until he had won his peace by right with his hard travail. And by the left-hand side is meant that the Father allowed his Son, willingly, to suffer in his manhood many pains without sparing him. And by his smock being almost in rags and tatters is understood the rods and scourges, the thorns and nails, the drawing and the dragging that rent his tender flesh. As I saw to some degree, his flesh was rent from the top of his head, falling in pieces until the time the bleeding ceased; and then it began to dry again, clinging to the bone. And by the wallowing and writhing, groaning and moaning, it is understood that he might never rise almightily from the time he had fallen into the Maiden's womb till his body was slain and dead; when he yielded his soul into the Father's hands with all humankind for whom he had been sent.

Julian spells out Christ's bodily sufferings in acute detail; but her purpose is fulfilled. By visualising the twofold identity of the servant, as both Son and Adam, she portrays a vivid image of Christ's Incarnation, the God-Man, enacting his saving task. It is a task he first performs alone, although as Man he acts for us all; now he invites Julian to join him in his working—an invitation open to all who are to follow him. Once he has finished his mortal task, the efficacy of his lifelong work and sufferings become apparent.

The harrowing of hell took place between Christ's death on Good Friday and his rising on the Sunday morning. During this time, he experienced the full weight of the world's sin, he was abandoned by his Father—*Eli, Eli, lama sabachthani*—he was literally in hell where he had come to claim his own.

At this point, he first began to show his might. For he went into hell, and when he was there he raised the great root out of the deep depths which rightfully were knit to him in high heaven. His body was in the grave until the Easter morrow, and from that time he never lay no more; for then truly was an end to the wallowing and writhing, the groaning and moaning; and our foul mortal flesh that God's Son took upon himself, which was Adam's old smock, strait, threadbare and short, then by our Saviour was made fair: now white, bright and of endless cleanness, wide and full, more fair, more rich than the clothing which I saw on the Father. For that clothing was blue and Christ's clothing is now fine and dazzling, a many-colour mix so marvellous it may not be described, it is so worshipful.

Christ, in becoming man, plunges himself into a knowledge of sin and its effect—obscuring, that is, his relationship with the Father. His descent into hell is the nadir of his entire earthly life: but by his suffering and death upon the cross, willingly endured, he is now empowered to rise anew. It is as if the very Trinity had ceased to function, yet now suddenly the Loving relationship between Father and Son has been restored in the Spirit. Perfect Love has finally overcome death.

Now the Lord no longer sits upon the earth in a wilderness, but he sits in his most noble throne which he made in heaven most to his liking.

Now the Son no longer stands before his Father in awe like a servant, poorly clothed, part naked; but he stands before the Father an equal, richly clad in generous bliss, and with a crown upon his head of

precious richness; for it was shown that we are his
crown, which is the Father's joy, the Son's glory, and
a liking to the Holy Spirit, and an endless marvellous
bliss to all who are in heaven.

Christ's work is done: in obedience to his Father, he has
willingly taken human flesh. It is the sinful stock of Adam,
yet by his earthly labours, above all by his painful obedience to death, he has 'raised the great root out of the
deep'. The Second Adam is now our Again-Maker offering
us his own New Life of Love. The servant who failed by
falling into the 'boggy dell' has been supplanted by the
Servant who is lovingly obedient, perfect in his redeeming
task of love.

Now the Son stands no more before the Father to his
left side like a labourer, but he is seated on his Father's
right hand in endless rest and peace. But this is not to
mean that the Son sits on the right hand, side by side,
as a man may sit beside his wife in this life: for there
is no such sitting, as I see it, in the Trinity; but he sits
on the Father's right hand, that is to say in the highest
nobility of the Father's joys.

Now is the spouse, God's Son, in peace with his
beloved wife who is the fair Maiden of endless joy.
And now the Son sits, true God and man, in his city of
rest and peace, which his Father has prepared for him
in his endless purpose: the Father in the Son and the
Holy Spirit in the Father and the Son.

'The Maiden of endless joy' represents the whole of humankind now reconciled and restored by Christ's saving purpose. The Maiden who becomes his mother by her 'yes'
cancels Eve's wanton disobedience. She also foreshadows
all who assent in like manner to God's loving approach. This
extended chapter with its elaborate solving of her parable

stands as a hinge to the whole text. The opening of the very next chapter reflects a fresh mood, a spirit of confidence: it seems as if a mist has lifted and Julian is now able to focus more clearly on the precise meaning of her showings, the amazing, neatly orchestrated plan of the Trinity's unfolding love to repair the damage sin has wrought in his human family.

And thus it was I saw that God rejoices that he is our Father, God rejoices that he is our Mother, and God rejoices that he is our true Spouse and our soul his beloved wife. And Christ rejoices that he is our Saviour.

I chose to begin, as it were, in the middle because I sense that this crucial chapter 51 illuminates all that Julian has to tell us. In a way, her experience is so overwhelming that it took much time and patient attending to deliberate her Lord's 'meaning'. We will follow her trail, listening and learning in her footsteps.

CHAPTER II

The dense and driven Passion, and frightful sweat...
G. M. Hopkins, *The Wreck of the Deutschland*

We return to Julian's opening text as she begins to relate her own detailed account of the seeming mortal sickness that laid her low in the week commencing 8 May 1373.

Then it suddenly came to me to ask for the second wound: that, by our Lord's gift and his own grace, I might truly feel his blissful passion. I simply wanted his pains to be my pains, such was my feeling for him; for now I could only long for God. But all the while I never looked for any vision or revelation: I simply wanted the same compassion that any good soul would have with our Lord Jesus who for love of us had willingly taken on our mortal flesh; and therefore I desired to suffer with him.

As chapter 4 opens, we have Julian's compassionate account of her First Showing. What is so striking is her bold approach: she speaks directly to her God, seeking to know him, to learn and understand. She will have her every petition plainly stated.

Now at once I saw red blood trickling down from under the garland. Hot and freely it fell, copious and real it was, as if it had just been pressed down upon his blessed head, who is truly both God and man, the very same that suffered thus for me. In that moment, I knew clearly that it was he himself who showed me, without intermediary of any kind.

She explains that as she lay dying:

My curate was called to be at my ending, and by the time he came I had set my eyes and might no longer speak. He set the cross before my face and said: 'I have brought you the image of your Maker and Saviour: look upon him and find your comfort there.'

I find Julian's self-effacement most endearing. She never for a moment anticipated any vision or revelation; and she considers her wish to suffer with Christ to be commonly held by anyone who pauses to consider how much he suffered for us. Throughout her entire account it is plain that Julian feels it her duty to share her experiences with 'all my even Christians'. It seems important, therefore, not to read her text objectively as a bystander, admiring her exposition, her flowing language. At once, I am drawn within her encounter, for plainly this is personally relevant to us all.

The crucifix faces us again and again, in chapels and churches and in our own homes. But how often do we truly face the dying Christ to ponder the enormity of his living love which he offers to each of us personally, today, right now? Julian's unassuming example offers us a fresh opportunity: not to pass by, or turn away, but to contemplate the inner reality of the dying Christ, enacting the stark reality of humankind—we are all born to die. Yet we are invited to die in his company. And I do not speak of my last moments, but of every moment given me. For we die every moment we live, stepping stones to that final leap into the darkness of faith to be welcomed by his open arms.

In a preliminary listing of the Sixteen Showings Julian tells us, that this first 'the precious crowning of our Lord with thorns... includes a showing of the Trinity with the Incarnation and tells of the unity between God and the soul... in which all the showings that follow are grounded and oned.' Indeed, the importance and complexity of her first showing is borne out by her treating it at length over the following six chapters.

Within this same showing, suddenly the Trinity filled my whole heart full of utmost joy. I knew then that heaven will be like this for all who come to it, without end:

> For the Trinity is God,
> and God is the Trinity.
> The Trinity is our Maker and Keeper,
> the Trinity is our everlasting Lover,
> everlasting joy and bliss, by our Lord Jesus Christ.

This was shown to me in the first and in all other showings: that where Jesus appears, the Blessed Trinity is understood. That is how I saw this showing.

And I exclaimed, 'Benedicite, Domine!'

I meant this greeting reverently, yet it came as a great shout. For I wanted to thank our Lord, who is so reverent, so holy and apart, for being so homely with a sinful creature who was still alive in this wretched flesh.

We will grow accustomed to Julian's ubiquitous treatment of the Trinity. While she does sometimes refer to God, most frequently she sees the Trinity working at every turn—'where Jesus appears, the Blessed Trinity is understood.' And nowhere is this more true than in his Passion. Jesus alone suffers: in his extremity, he is abandoned. And yet, it is the Trinity that is expressing God's absolute and unchanging love for humankind in the Person of the suffering Christ. And it is the working out of Christ's Passion that will continue in every human soul to come, for the

Trinity is working 'through mercy and grace' in the story of humankind.

And Julian is continually stressing this intimacy of the Trinity with the human soul. 'Homely' and most frequently 'courteous' are Julian's words describing God's dealings with her. While conscious of God's ever-present, wooing love, she never loses her sense of reverent gratitude towards her Maker. The story of this first showing continues:

Next he brought our blessed Lady to my understanding. I saw her with my understanding as though she were with me physically: a simple maid and meek, so young she seemed like a mere child—yet the very same age when she conceived. And God showed me then something of the wisdom and truth of her soul. In particular, I saw her attitude toward her Maker, how she marvelled with great reverence, when he wished to be born of her, who was a mere simple creature he himself had made. It was this wisdom, this truth, seeing how great was her Maker compared to her own littleness, which made her say to Gabriel, 'Behold me, God's handmaid'.

Then I knew for certain that she was more worthy and more full of grace than all the rest of God's creation, with the sole exception of the manhood of Christ.

Julian sees Mary as pre-eminent in the human race; for she is the first human person to utter a unique 'Yes!' to God's love. And her *Fiat* enables a second Person to do likewise, the Christ Man himself. Thus Mary is called to be the Second Eve: her Son, the new Adam. Yet she is also the model for us all; her *Fiat* becomes our 'yes!' as we welcome God's gift of his Spirit into our hearts.

Irenæus, writing barely a century after Christ's death declares: 'The Word, only Son of the Father, is ever present to mankind, he is one with the work that he has fashioned in his Father's knowledge: for he has impregnated it with his own divine seed (1 Jn 3:9)'.

Julian will expand this notion, she names it 'the working': the dynamic activity of the Trinity in the human soul is a love relationship to which we are continually prompted to respond by grace. And so each person is fashioning their own unique expression of Christ's work on earth.

It is like a young pianist performing her interpretation of a Nocturne by Chopin or Brahms' last Rhapsody. The music she is playing belongs to the creativity of its composer; at the same time, she is inspired by that same person's gift as she brings her own talent to the keyboard— to the delight of her attentive audience.

[5]

While I still had sight of our Lord's head as it bled, he showed me a further understanding of his homely love. I saw that he is the ground of all that is good and supporting for us. He is our clothing that lovingly wraps and folds us about; it embraces us and closes us all around as it hangs upon us with such tender love; for truly he can never leave us. This made me see that he is for us everything that is good.

At the same time, he showed me something small, about the size of a hazelnut, that seemed to lie in the palm of my hand as round as a tiny ball. I tried to understand the sight of it, wondering what it could possibly mean. The answer came: 'This is all that is made.'

I felt it was so small that it could easily fade to nothing; but again I was told, 'This lasts and it will go on lasting forever because God loves it. And so it is with every being that God loves.'

Julian's hazelnut, like her non-existent cat, is frequently glossed over with a certain amount of sentimentality. But with her habitual attention to detail, she has over the years come to penetrate its rich symbolism. The sum of all creation dwindles to the size of a hazelnut when compared to the majesty of its Creator. The marvellous realisation of her Maker, her Keeper, her Lover she finds overwhelming: and no creature or created thing can come between them. 'Our hearts are restless until they rest in You', cries Augustine. And Julian echoes this refrain with feeling.

I saw three properties about this tiny object. First, God made it: second, God loves it; and third, that God keeps it. Yet what this really means to me, that he is the Maker, the Keeper, the Lover, I cannot begin to tell. For until I am fully one with him, I can never have full rest nor true bliss; that is to say, until I am so at one with him that no created thing comes between us, my God and me.

We must come to realize this: created things are nothing, and we must turn aside from them to love and have our God who is not made. This is the only reason why we are not fully at ease in heart and soul: that we look to find our true rest in these things that are so little that they contain no rest. And we know not our God, who is almighty, all wise, all good. For he is the very rest.

This 'indifference' to created things is a key-note in *The Spiritual Exercises* of Saint Ignatius. In his opening salvo of the First Week, Ignatius sets out the 'Principle and Foundation', the building block of our approach to God, or rather enabling us to recognise and receive his love. The human race is created to praise, reverence and serve God; all created things are to be seen as means to this end. Julian presses the same argument in warmer vein as she sees creation from God's point of view; and she concludes with a poignant prayer.

God will be known; he is pleased when we find our rest in him. All that falls short of him will never satisfy us. This is why no soul can be at peace until it is rid of all created things. Only when the soul turns away and denies itself so as to find him, who is All, will it be able to receive true peace and rest.

And I saw quite clearly how much God is pleased when a person comes to him in all simplicity, as it were quite naked, unafraid and trusting. This is the kind yearnings of the soul as it is touched by the Holy Spirit, according to the understanding I have of this showing:

> God, of your goodness, give me yourself;
> for you are enough to me;
> I may nothing ask that is less that may be full worship to you.
> And if I ask anything that is less,
> I am ever left wanting;
> but only in you I have all.

These words are full lovesome to the soul and closely touch the will of God and his goodness. For his goodness fills all his creatures and spills into all that he does. He is our endless home: he only made us for himself; he remakes us by his blessed passion and always keeps us in his blessed love.

All this is down to his goodness.

[6]

Julian will deal with prayer at greater length in later chapters; for now she is content to emphasise that all prayer is God's initiative. Busyness is no part of our praying. She rises to her most eloquent as she tells of God's loving intimacy with us all, for he is pure goodness.

I understood this revelation to teach our soul to cling fast to the goodness of God. At the same time, I remembered all the different ways we are accustomed to pray and how busy we become when we lose sight of how God loves us. For I was persuaded at this time that what pleases God, what delights him most, is when we pray simply trusting in his goodness...

For the goodness of God is our highest prayer, and it comes down to us to meet our least need. It quickens our soul and brings it to life; it makes it grow in grace and virtue; moreover it is nearest in kind [i.e. nature/ our human nature] and readiest in grace; the very same grace the soul hungers after now and always, until we know him verily that has us all in himself beclosed.

Just as the body is clad in clothes and the flesh in skin and the bones in flesh with the heart in the breast, so are we, soul and body, clothed and wrapped around in the goodness of God. Yet it is even more intimate than this, because they all disappear once they decay. But the goodness of God is always whole and more near to us without any comparison. It is true that our Lover desires the soul to stay close to him with all its strength, clinging ever more tightly to his goodness.

Of all things the heart may think, this pleases God the most and affords us much progress. Our soul is loved so preciously by him, our highest good, that it is beyond all human understanding. In truth, no human alive can fathom how much, how sweetly and tenderly, our Maker loves us. And so we are able by the help of his grace to stay beholding in prayer this lofty, surpassing and immeasurable love that almighty God has toward us of his goodness.

And this means that we may ask our Lover with reverence anything we wish for our dearest kindly wish is to have God, and his good will is to have us. Nor can we cease in our desire to love and have him until it is fulfilled in endless joy. Then we will want no more.

[7]

Wishing to teach us this important lesson, as it seemed to me, our Lord God showed me our lady Saint Mary, as she was at that time, that is to say the high wisdom and truth she had as she beheld her Maker, he being so great. This greatness and the nobility of her contemplating God filled her full of holy dread, and by comparison she saw herself so little and so low, so simple and so poor in regard to her Lord God, that this reverend dread also filled her with meekness. This then was the ground by which she was filled all full of grace with every kind of virtue overpassing all creatures.

Once again we see how Julian is taught to regard Mary: not as someone holy and aloof, but as one of us. As it has already been said, Mary is our human exemplar; so that our response to God's love needs to be equally unconditional.

But Julian is still vividly aware of the central dynamic of Christ's passion in communicating God's loving purpose to mankind.

And all the while he showed me this (as I said before, in a spiritual way), I could see a bodily vision of his head bleeding freely. Great drops of blood fell from under the garland; like pellets they were of reddish brown, for the bleeding was copious; but when they began to spread, they seemed to turn to bright red. As they reached the eyebrows, suddenly they vanished...

This showing was vivid and lifelike, hideous and dreadful, sweet and lovely. But of all the things I saw, this was my greatest comfort: that our good Lord, who is so holy and so much to be feared, is at the same instant so homely and so courteous. This warmed me full of love and comforted my very soul.

Julian's encounter with her suffering Christ reflects his mother's attitude—that of a powerless creature face to face with her almighty Maker. At the same time, there comes the overwhelming awareness, as Julian puts it, of his 'homely and courteous' love.

The following chapter is a recapitulation of all that comprises this her First Showing; but Julian's urgent message is one of self-effacement. She receives her Revelation, then it fades—'I was left with a spiritual vision in my understanding...' 'All the while I felt great love toward all my fellow Christians for I wanted them all to share my understanding of everything I saw—I knew it would comfort them. And I felt sure that this revelation was for all the world to see.'

The mark of true contemplatives is that they hold a genuine concern for mankind at large. While Julian's message appears to have had a limited circulation after her death, it has taken 600 years for its full impact to arrive. And one cannot but wonder at the timing. In Julian's days her message of God's goodness and his unceasing love for mankind was sorely needed: today, it would seem, we are never more in need.

[9]

I myself am not a good person merely because I received these showings; they will only make me a better Christian if I come to love God more. And inasmuch as you come to a greater love of God through them, then will you profit more than I. Here I am not talking to the wise, who already know as much, but to simple folk, for your help and comfort. For in truth, I was never shown that God loved me more than the least soul that stands in his grace; indeed I am certain there be many who have had neither sight nor showing save that of the common teaching of holy Church, yet they love God better than I. For when I look to myself as a single individual, then I am nothing. But all my hopes come from being united in one love with all my fellow Christians. For on this unity the life of all that shall be saved depends.

[10] THE SECOND SHOWING

At first reading, Julian's experience seems so intense as to belong to her alone. Yet immediately she draws us into 'the working', that is to say the common Christian calling to identify with the suffering humanity of Christ, especially to 'see him continually'. And we must 'seek with a will gladly and merrily'; and all the while though 'his working is secret ... yet he will be perceived.'

After this, as I saw with bodily sight the face of the crucifix that hung before me, which I beheld continually, a part of his passion; contempt, spitting, soiling and buffeting as well as many distressing pains—more than I can tell—and frequent changing of colour...

I saw this bodily, yet it was dark and mournful, so that I wanted more light in order to see it more clearly. And I was answered in my reason: 'If God will show you more, he shall be your light.' For I saw him, yet I sought him.

For we are so blind here, so unwise, that we can never seek God until in his goodness he shows himself to us. And if we glimpse him through grace, then are we stirred by the same grace to seek him with great desire so as to see him more blissfully.

And thus I saw him and I sought him; I had him, yet I wanted him. And this is and should be our common working in this life, as I see it...He wants us to believe that we see him continually, even though it seems to us that we see him very little, since in this way he will make us daily grow in grace. For he will be seen and he will be sought; he will be waited for and he will be trusted.

Here is a typical example of Julian's deliberate choice of word, delighting in double meanings that stress her point: 'he *will* be seen...' Will as a promise of something that will come to pass: but also he wills it to be.

The experience of her Showings is now twenty or more years into the past, but she retains her spiritual memory of their vivid message. And yet frequently they fade, and she begs for more light. At once, she sees that this is all the gift of God and working out his plan with all mankind.

Now I wish to tell of the understanding I have come to by God's grace.

We know in our faith and through our belief in the teaching and preaching of the holy Church that the

blessed Trinity made humanity to his image and in his
likeness. In the same manner we know that humankind fell by sin so wretchedly and so deeply that there
was no other way to restore us than by him who made
us. He who made humankind by love, in the same love
would restore us to the same bliss, even overpassing
it.

'Overpassing': a verbal signature peculiar to Julian is her
'wordknot', when she skilfully presses her chosen word for
more than one meaning. In Middle English overpass means
surpass. But invert it to Passover: Pascal Christ, our Again-
Maker, brings us superabundant gifts far surpassing those
originally offered to Adam and Eve. And as a sub-plot to
her narrative lies the continual promise of the parable of
the lord and his servant which we have savoured but which
Julian chooses to hold back until the very centre of her
work.

For just as we were made like to the Trinity in our first
making, our Maker wants us to be like Jesus Christ our
Saviour, in heaven without end, by virtue of our
again-making.

We return to Julian's teaching on prayer, namely her
distinction between seeking and beholding. The former
refers to our attending to God's continuous presence, the
latter to the experience of contemplation—God's gift of his
loving Spirit.

By this sight I was taught to understand that our soul's
continual seeking pleases God greatly; for we can do
no more than seek, suffer and trust, and it is worked
in the soul by the Holy Spirit; and when we find him
clearly this is by special grace at a time he chooses.
Seeking with faith, hope and charity pleases our Lord;

and finding pleases the soul and fills it full of joy. And so I was taught to understand that seeking is as good as beholding all the while he allows the soul to labour. It is God's will that we continue to seek him and strive to behold him, waiting for the moment when he chooses by special grace to show us himself. This does him the most honour and profits you; it happens gently and effectively with the guiding grace of the Holy Spirit. For when a soul fastens itself to God, truly trusting, whether in seeking or beholding, this is the best service it may render him, as I see it.

We know he will appear suddenly and blissfully to all his lovers; for his working is secret, yet he will be perceived, and his appearing will be swift and sudden; and he will be trusted, for he is full gracious and homely—blessed may he be!

This distinction between seeking and beholding is dear to Julian. It perfectly expresses the 'weal and woe' she experiences in her daily life. A small child finds comfort in his mother's arms; he loves to be cuddled, but he may not stay here all day.

[11] THE THIRD SHOWING

So far Julian's revelations have centred on the suffering Christ who shows us the full extent of God's outstretched loving arms towards humankind. We now have a complete reversal of perspective: Julian is shown God's powerful workings within all that he has made. But immediately she is confused by the nature of sin. If God is at work in all things, where does sin come in? This is a problem she will wrestle with at length in later chapters.

After this I saw God in a point, that is to say in my understanding, and in this sight I saw that he is in all things. I beheld attentively, seeing and knowing in the sight. And as I marvelled quietly, a soft dread came over me so that I asked in my mind, 'what is sin?' For I saw clearly that God does all things, even the very least. I knew truly that nothing happens by chance or accident, but all is by the foreseeing wisdom of God. Even if it seems by chance or accident in our sight, that is due to blindness or short-sightedness on our part. For these things are in God's foreseeing wisdom from without beginning (indeed he leads them all rightfully, gloriously, continually to their best end); yet as they come about, they fall upon us suddenly to take us unawares. And thus, by our blindness and lack of foresight, we see them as mishaps or accidents; but it is not like that with God. Therefore, I needs must recognize that all that is done, it is well done, for our Lord does all. But at this time, creatures' deeds were not shown, but only our Lord working in the creature. For he is the midpoint of all things and he does all things; yet I was sure he did not sin. And here I saw truly that sin is no-deed, for in all this sin was never shown. I could no longer marvel at this but beheld our Lord and whatever he would show me.

As she 'quietly marvels', she is overwhelmed by her own lowliness. Just as Mary asked 'how might this be?' so Julian questions the conundrum—if 'God does all thing', how can he be a party to mankind's sinfulness. And her answer comes 'sin is no-deed'. Both Augustine and Aquinas after him took the same stand on sin. While God is pure active Love, sin is a black hole. Sin, while obscuring his love, may never obliterate it. There will be further deliberations on the reality of sin which leads to Julian's theology of 'the two wills'. For now, she continues:

For a while, therefore, the rightful workings of God were shown to this soul. Rightfulness has two fair properties: it is right and it is full. And even so are all the works of God our Lord; and to them belongs neither the work of mercy nor grace, for where nothing fails, all is right.

Now this vision was shown to my understanding, for our Lord wants the soul truly turned so as to behold him and all his works in general. For they are full of goodness, all his doings are easy and sweet; and at once the soul is eased when it turns from our own blind judgement toward the fair, sweet judgement of God.

While to us some deeds may seem well done, others evil, this is not so in God's sight. For since all things have their ground in God's making, so all that is done belongs to God's doing. It is easy to understand that the best things are well done; yet as equally well as the best and highest deed is done, so too is the least thing well done; and all because it belongs to the order God ordained from without beginning, for he is the only doer... Thus no single thing shall fail at the point that he made them all fully good; therefore the blessed Trinity is always fully pleased in all his works. And all this he showed most blissfully, and this was his meaning:

> See I am God.
> See I am in all thing.
> See I do all thing.
> See I never lift my hands off my own works, nor ever shall, without end.

See I lead all thing to the end I ordained for it from without beginning with the same might, wisdom and love that I made it.
How should anything be amiss?

Thus mightily, wisely and lovingly was the soul examined in this vision. Then I saw truly that I needs must assent with great reverence, simply enjoying in God.

At times, Julian seems to run away with herself, such is her apparent eagerness to stress the positive. But she has been shown the world's workings from God's viewpoint. 'See I never lift my hands off my own works...' God delights in every detail of his creation. He is fully active throughout world history, his hands in the dough, as it were. From our human perspective, the story of mankind is shot through with pain, suffering and contradictions. But our Maker is at the helm in spite of all this: 'how should anything be amiss?'

So ends this single chapter dealing with her Third Showing. It embodies precisely Julian's experience of 'beholding', when, as it were, God takes the reins and holds the soul in his Being. Then the human soul is truly itself, 'buxom' and unresisting to God's courteous Love. In Middle English, *buxum* means meek, pleasing, obliging, gracious: the qualities of Mary which we are to follow.

[12] THE FOURTH SHOWING

Only three women friends of Jesus and just a single disciple were courageous enough to witness the torments of his death upon the cross. Julian has already told how she wished 'to be like Mary Magdalene and others who were Christ's lovers ... the compassion of our Lady ...that saw his pains at that time'. In this Fourth Showing We encounter once again the suffering Christ, this time focussing on his Precious Blood. Her vision offers a gruesome portrayal of the dying Christ which we flinch from. And yet the true images of today's wars, famines and revolutions are just as terrifying: they too are sanitised for our TV screens.

After this I saw in my beholding that the body seemed to be bleeding plenteously due to the scourging. And this is how it looked: the fair skin was deeply broken into the tender flesh with the sharp beating all across the sweet body; so plenteously did the hot blood run out that there was neither skin nor even wound, but it seemed as if it were all blood.

The forcefulness of Julian's text in this florid passage must be understood in the context of its compounded origins. Firstly, she is at death's door and doubtless delirious with a high temperature; and in the midst of what is thought of as her final moments, she suffers a series of visions. Later, she recovers and makes her first record of these over-whelming events. Finally, after decades of prayer and pondering, she brings together both her definitive account and her conclusions as to their 'meaning'. Fact and meta-phor abound for this one end.

And when it came to the point where it should have spilled down, then it vanished; notwithstanding, the bleeding continued for a while when it could be seen by looking closely. And this seemed so plenteous to me that I thought if it had been real and actually happening, then it would have soaked the bed in blood and spilled over all around.

Then I was reminded how God had made the waters of the earth so plentiful in our service to meet our bodily comfort, all for tender love that he has for us; yet he likes it better that we take his blessed blood quite naturally to wash away sin. There is no liquid made that he prefers to give us, by virtue of the blessed Godhead. It is our birthright and blissfully flows to us by virtue of his precious love. The dear and worthy blood of our Lord Jesus Christ, as truly as it is most precious, so truly is it plentiful. Behold and see: this precious and plenteous, worthy and dear blood descends down into hell, bursts forth her bonds and delivers all there who belong to the court of heaven.

'It is our birthright': *'it is our kinde'* that is belonging to us by our very nature.

One might speculate whether Julian ever received the Sacrament under both kinds as is our privilege today.

The harrowing of hell was a familiar image in medieval times being a frequent subject for church murals. Christ is depicted descending into hell to redeem Adam and Eve and all the souls awaiting his resurrection on the third day—'leading captives in your train' (Ps 68:18).

[13] THE FIFTH SHOWING

After this, without any words, God allowed me to behold him for a considerable time, taking in all I had seen, understanding all that was contained therein, as much as my simple soul might. And then without voice or any opening of lips, there formed in my soul these words: 'Here is how the fiend is overcome.'

In this our Lord showed that his blessed passion is the overcoming of the fiend. God showed that the fiend has the same malice now as before the Incarnation; and yet although he labours as hard now, he continually sees all those saved souls escape him, wonderfully by virtue of Christ's precious passion. This means he has as much sorrow when God permits him to work as when he is prevented; and he can never do so much evil as he wishes, for God has taken his power up into his own hands. For as I see it, there can be no wrath with God, for he is our endless Lord, having regard to his own honour as well as the profit of all who will be saved.

'There can be no wrath in God': a key-note to Julian's revelation—God is all active Love. He may only regard and receive us in Love, the same Love by which he is 'Again-Making us'.

She is acutely aware of the power of 'the fiend' which she experiences in several alarming visitations; but she is far more confident in the all-conquering power of Christ given to us—'in mercy and grace'—by means of his passion and death.

Also I saw how our Lord scorns his malice and deadens his might, and he wills us to do the same. And at this sight I laughed so mightily that I made those standing around laugh with me. And although I did not see Christ laugh, yet I understood that we might rightly laugh, comforting ourselves and finding our joy in God because the devil is overcome.

[14] THE SIXTH SHOWING

After this our good Lord said, 'I thank you for your labour, namely that of your youth.' At this my under-standing was lifted up to heaven, where I saw our Lord as a Lord in his own house to which he has called all his most dear servants and friends to a solemn feast. I saw the Lord take no place of honour in his house, rather I saw him rule royally there, filling it full of joy and mirth. For it is to see the glorious Godhead in this way, face to face, that fills the very heavens with such joy and bliss.

God showed three degrees of bliss that belong to every soul in heaven who has served God in any way here on earth. The first is that thanks and due honour they will receive from our Lord God as soon as they are delivered from their pain; this thanks is so high and so heaped with honour that it seems as if it would quite fill them even were they to receive no more. The second is that all the blessed already in heaven will see this worshipful thanks as he makes his servant known to them all. And the third is that, as new and pleasing as the thanks may be when first received, just so it shall continue to last without end. And I saw how homely and sweetly this was shown: that the life story of everyone shall be told in heaven and each shall be rewarded for the loyal service given through their days.

And so the more a loving soul sees this courtesy of God, the more gladly will they serve him all the days of their life.

No wonder Julian appears to long for her future heaven. She lived in dangerous and turbulent times. Europe was only just recovering from the ravages of the Black Death. Serious social upheaval erupted in 1381 when Watt Tyler led his peasant army into London.

They stormed the Tower of London, executing the Chancellor Simon of Sudbury, the Archbishop of Canterbury, who had been responsible for the Poll Tax, the initial cause of the uprising. In Norwich, Geoffrey Litster, raised a similar band of protesters. They took over the Castle where they forced several noblemen to wait upon them. The City was paralysed for two weeks until Henry le

Despenser, the warring bishop of Norwich, defeated the rabble at North Walsham.

More pertinent to Julian herself was the church's continuing efforts to combat the Lollard movement. An early foretaste of the Reformers of the 16th Century, their followers met for worship in secret, reading from an English translation of The Bible. In Julian's day, such translations were forbidden as was worship apart from the Church. Lollards were hunted down, tried for heresy: the penalty for the guilty was death by fire. The so-called 'Lollards Pit' where these gruesome executions took place was a few hundred paces from Julian's cell. This also raises the question: how would Julian's text been viewed in her day had it seen the light of day. The Carmelite Thomas Netter was an energetic pursuivant of both Lollards and the followers of Wycliffe who was born two years after Julian's showings. I suspect he would have found plenty to wonder at in her writings: not only was she a woman, but she had no formal mandate to teach.

[15] THE SEVENTH SHOWING

Julian is puzzled by experiencing alternative feelings of 'weal and woe', especially since they appear to have no connection to any sin on her part. She concludes that this simple condition of human life is the way our Lord awakens the depths of our feeling soul to open to his Love. Yet in his apparent absence, he is no less present as steadily we awaken to his continuous Love.

I well remember the shock and puzzlement when, three weeks into my Jesuit noviceship, I suddenly found myself heavy-hearted and downcast for no apparent reason. But there is no reason for the sun to go in save that a cloud has momentarily shaded it. God seems to withdraw so that we may stand alone until we experience his return; and yet, of course, he is never absent for one single blink of the eye.

Julian takes to her anchorhold, full of her strange experience. But as time passes, she must learn to bear the ups and downs of everyday life.

After this he showed me a sovereign spiritual loving in my soul. I was filled full of everlasting sureness that took hold of me in power without pain or dread. The feeling was so glad and so spiritual that I was in all peace and rest, so that nothing on earth might grieve me. Yet this lasted but a while; then I was changed, left to myself with all the heaviness and weariness of life—I was burdened with myself, so that I barely had patience to live. There was no comfort, no ease: only faith, hope and charity; and while I had these in reality, yet they were little in feeling. But soon enough our blessed Lord once again gave me that comfort and rest of soul, lovingly and surely. And then I was shown once again that pain of feeling; then the loving joy: now the one, now the other, many times repeating—I suppose some twenty in all.

This vision was shown to my understanding that it is necessary for some souls to feel this way, sometime in comfort and sometime failing, left all alone to themselves. For God wants us to know that it is he who keeps us surely whether we be in woe or weal. And for the good of our soul we are sometimes left to ourselves, without sin being always the cause; for at this time I had not sinned, for it was all so sudden, yet I was still left to myself. Equally, I did not deserve to have received all these feelings of bliss.

When it pleases him, our Lord gives freely of himself, and then sometimes he suffers us to feel in woe. Yet both are one and the same love; for it is God's will that we hold ourselves in his comfort with all our might. For bliss will last without end while pain passes and will be brought to nothing for those that shall be saved. And therefore it is not God's will that we linger in feelings of pain by mourning or sorrowing over them, yet we should swiftly pass them by, keeping ourselves in his endless love.

[16] THE EIGHTH SHOWING

After this Christ showed a part of his passion near his death. I saw his sweet face as it was then, all dry and bloodless with the pallor of dying. And by degrees it grew still more pale, dead and listless; and then, as it became almost lifeless, turning to blue. After this, as death itself approached, the flesh turned from blue to brown. His passion was shown me in his face and in particular his lips; where before they were fresh and ruddy and pleasing to my sight, I now saw only these four colours...

The modern reader will flinch at these intimate details of the dying Christ as Julian continues her description. But remember her initial petition, that she should have mind of his passion in the same way as those who saw him die on Calvary. And there is a further consideration: in Julian's time, affective spirituality as taught by Bonaventure in the previous century had caught on. The penitent was encouraged to visualize in detail the sufferings of Christ in order to share his merits. And so the next two chapters continue in similar vein...

In all this time of Christ's pain I felt nothing other than for his pains. Until I thought to myself: 'Little did I realize what pain it was I asked for,' and like a wretch I regretted it, thinking to myself, if only I had known what it were like, I would never have prayed for it. For I thought these pains of mine surpassed even those of bodily death, saying to myself, 'is there any pain like this?' And the answer came into my head: 'Hell is another pain apart, for there is despair. But of all pains that lead to salvation, this pain is the most: to see your love suffer.' How might any pain be more to me than to see him who is my whole life, my bliss and all my joy suffer?

[18] Stabat Mater dolorosa juxta Crucem lacrimosa, dum pendebat Filius.

In chapter eighteen, Julian develops her meditation on Christ's sufferings by considering his mother's own pains as she stood below her dying son while he bled to death: and such pains belong also to us and to all humankind.

Here I saw some part of the compassion of our Lady St Mary. For Christ and she were so united in love that the greatness of his loving was to cause her very great pain: in this I saw a substance of kind love that creatures have toward him, continued by grace. And this human love was generously, overpassingly shown in his sweet mother; for since she loved him more than all others, her pains exceeded theirs.

'A substance of kind love': Julian, the theologian, is making a bold and original connection between our 'kind' or human nature which Christ has received from his mother taking it as his own and our loving response to his Incarnation—that is grounded in kind and continued by grace. As his mother, Mary has a unique compassion for his sufferings; yet through that same kin(d)ship with him, we too have a similar 'kind love' [rooted in our human nature] that may be perfected by grace.

And in this I saw a great oneing between Christ and ourselves; I knew it to be so: for when he was in pain, we were in pain. And all creatures able to suffer suffered pain with him—I am talking about all those creatures that God made to our service. The whole firmament, and the earth itself, throughout its whole nature, failed for sorrow at the time of Christ's dying. For it belonged to the nature of all things to know he was their God, since in him stood their whole strength. When he failed, it was only natural that they must fail with him, as far as they might, sorrowing at his pains. And so too those that were his friends suffered for their love of him—as they felt the loss of comfort from God's inner keeping.

And so our Lord was made nothing for us, and in this way we all stand as nothing with him; and shall do until we come to his bliss, as I shall now tell.

[19]

In this chapter, we have first mention of Julian's teaching of the Two Wills, 'the outward and the inner'. She distinguishes between our inner substance and our outer sensuality; this is developed further in chapters 37 and 55. For now she is aware of her waywardness in regretting her prayer to suffer Christ's pains with him; yet this belongs to her weakness of 'mortal flesh', our sensuality. But her steadfast intention remains firm: she has chosen to be with Christ 'as her heaven'. The inner will overrules any outer human weakness, the power of Christ at work.

At this time, I wanted to look away from the cross, yet I dared not do so. For I knew well that all the while I beheld the cross, I was sure and safe. Then a suggestion came to mind: 'Look up to heaven, to his Father'. And then I was sure in my faith that there was nothing between the cross and heaven that could draw me aside. I answered for myself inwardly with every power in my soul, saying, 'No, I may not, for you are my heaven'. For I knew well enough that since it was he who bound me so sore, then would he unbind me as and when he willed.

Thus I was taught to choose Jesus to be my heaven, whom at that time I could only see in pain. And that lesson has served me that I should do so evermore, choosing only Jesus for my heaven in weal and woe. And though, wretch as I am, I repented my prayer (I said before that if I had known what this pain would mean, I would have been unwilling to pray for it), here I saw clearly that it was only the complaining of weak flesh without assent of the soul; and in this God assigns no blame. Repenting and deliberate choice are two separate things, and I felt them both at the same time; for they belong to two different aspects, the outward and the inner. The outward part is our mortal flesh, which is presently in pain and woe. It was this that weighed on me heavily at this time. This part, it was, repented. The inner part is a high and blissful life all at peace and kept in love; and this was felt more secretly; and within this part I did choose Jesus to be my heaven, mightily, wisely and with all my will. And in this I saw in truth that the inward part is master and lord over the outer, neither regarding nor taking heed to it, but all the effort of will is set steadfastly to join with our Lord Jesus. I was not shown that the outer should draw the inner to assent; but that the inner draws the outer by grace, and both will be oned in bliss without end by the power of Christ: this was I shown.

[20]

And thus I saw our Lord Jesus lingering a long while; for the unity with the Godhead gave strength to the manhood to suffer in love more than anyone else might suffer. By that I mean not only more pain than anyone at all might suffer, but also that he suffered more pain than the whole of humanity from the first to the last day of salvation, considering the worth of this highest, most honourable king and his shameful, cruel and painful death. For he that is highest and most worthy was completely humiliated and utterly despised. Indeed the highest point in the passion is to think and know who it is that suffered.

He suffered for us just as long as it was possible for him to suffer, but now he is risen up, he no longer suffers; yet still he suffers with us. I beheld all this by his grace, and I saw how his love for our soul is so strong that he chose firmly with great resolve to suffer all mildly, making light of what he paid. Thus the soul touched by this grace beholds the very truth: that the pains of Christ's passion pass all pain. Yet I say these pains shall be turned into everlasting great joys by virtue of Christ's passion.

[21]

I saw the truth in this that if he were to show himself to us now, no pain imaginable that could fall our way on earth or elsewhere would trouble us, for everything would be to our joy and happiness. But instead he offers us some measure of the passion that he himself suffered in his own life. We are afflicted by his own cross and so we suffer with him, as is our human lot. And his reason for our suffering in this way: he wants of his goodness to make us heirs with him in his bliss. As our reward for the little pain we suffer here, we will know God himself without end, which otherwise we might never have. And the greater are our pains with him on his cross, the greater will be our reward with him when we come into his kingdom.

'The problem of pain' has been a constant stumbling block to believers and humanists alike: why did God allow the Holocaust, how can he stand by as children are abused by priests? Julian accepts human suffering, even at its most extreme, as our human lot. Christ's suffering and humiliating death is terrible to behold: but 'we are afflicted by his own cross and so we suffer with him'. It is false to see Christ's passion apart from the tragedy of human suffering: he is incorporated, literally, in every human situation, good or evil. He continues to suffer in and with us.

[22] THE NINTH SHOWING

Then our good Lord asked me, 'Are you pleased I suffered for you?' I said, 'Yes, dear Lord, in your mercy: yes, good Lord, bless you always.' Then our good Lord Jesus replied, 'If you are pleased, then I too am pleased. This is my joy, my bliss, my endless liking that I was ever able to suffer for you. For truly, if I could have suffered more, I would have suffered more.'

As I attended to this, my understanding was lifted into heaven, where I saw three heavens ... each one belonging to the blessed manhood of Christ. In the first heaven, Christ showed me his Father—not in bodily vision, but in his property and in his working; that is to say, I saw in Christ that his Father is.

The working of the Father is this: he gives his Son, Jesus Christ, a prize. This gift and prize is so great a reward to Jesus that his Father could give him none better or more pleasing to him. The first heaven is his rewarding his Father, for the Father is greatly pleased with everything Jesus has done toward our salvation. So that we are not merely his by his buying, but, by the courteous gift of the Father, we are equally his happiness, we are his prize, we are his crown.

And now as I thought about his blessed passion, I began also to understand about the second heaven: for his love that brought him to suffer exceeds his pain as much as heaven is above the earth. This was the love that prompted him to tell me, 'If I could suffer more, I would suffer more.'

Now I will tell of the third heaven which I saw in the passion—namely, the joy and the happiness that makes him like it. For we are his bliss; in us he takes his liking without end and so shall we in him, with his grace. And all this began at the sweet Incarnation, lasting to the day when he rose again on Easter day; this was the extent and the reckoning of the work that made our redemption come about. In this work he finds his endless joy.

All the Trinity worked together in the passion of Christ, affording us the generous power of his abundant grace. While it was only he, Mary's Son, that suffered, yet all the Trinity rejoice in it without end.

[24] THE TENTH SHOWING

With joyful face our good Lord looked down at his side and I was invited by his tender gaze to ponder this wound. For there within, he showed a place that was inviting fair; and large enough it was to offer refuge for all who will be saved, there to find their rest in peace and love. And with this sweet beholding he brought to mind his most dear blood and the precious water which he let pour from his side, all of his love. And looking with him, I realised that his heart was indeed broken in two. Now with his tender look he revealed something of God's inner bliss, as my soul was led in some measure to know his never-ending love, flowing from before time to the present and for all eternity. And with this our good Lord gently spoke: 'Lo, how I loved you.' It was as if he had said, 'My darling, behold and see your Lord, and your God, who is your Maker and your endless joy; see what liking and bliss I have in your salvation, and for my love enjoy now with me.'

CHAPTER III

Thus far, Julian's Showings have centred upon the sufferings of Christ; the remaining six revelations cover a range of subjects—Our Lady, prayer, the nature of sin and how God, the Trinity, deals lovingly with the human soul. The right moment, perhaps, to pause and reflect on our best approach to this complex work, if we are to gain the most from it.

On first coming to Julian's text, it is easy to read it as one continuing narrative describing her experiences as it were in the present. This would be misleading in the extreme, for they are shot through with reflections that would have been inserted and modified, possibly more than once, over a period of twenty years and more. But the key to our successfully assimilating Julian's inner meaning as a whole is to take her at her word that these showings were not something private for us to wonder at from afar, but that they are relevant to 'all my even Christians'. As she has already assured us in Chapter 9:

> I myself am not a good person merely because I received these showings; they will only make me a better Christian if I come to love God more. And inasmuch as you come to a greater love of God through them, then will you profit more than I.

[25] THE ELEVENTH SHOWING

His face still full of mirth and joy, our Lord now looked down to his right side, and I was reminded where our Lady stood all the while he suffered on his cross. And he said, 'Will you see her?' ... I answered saying, 'Yes, dear Lord, in your mercy: yes, good Lord, if it be your will.'

After his own self, she is the most blissful sight. Yet just because of that, I am not taught that I should long to see her bodily presence while I am here, but simply the good virtues of her holy soul—her truth, her wisdom and her love.

Visions of Our Lady remain a preoccupation of the Catholic Church, that is to say they appear to erupt from the lay soul. Lourdes, Fatima, Knock: Julian's seeking turns aside from mere physical showings to penetrate the essence of his Mother's crucial role in Christ's working, the working to which we are all invited and with which we remain involved.

Oftentimes I prayed for this, to see her in her bodily presence, but I never saw her so. But I was shown her in a spiritual way, three times: the first as a maiden when she first conceived, the second when she mourned beneath the cross, and third, as she now is, full of liking, joy and honour.

[26] THE TWELFTH SHOWING

After this our Lord revealed himself even more glorified than I had seen before. And then I knew that our soul will never be at rest until it comes into him: then will we know him as our true life and be filled with his joy, his happiness and his courteous homeliness.
And now our Lord repeated many times:

> I it am, I it am
> I it am that is highest
> I it am that you love
> I it am that you like
> I it am that you serve
> I it am that you long for
> I it am that you desire
> I it am that you mean

I it am that is all
I it am that holy Church preaches and teaches you
I it am that showed myself to you here

His words were so many that I could never hope to take them all in…

Here is Julian 'beholding'. She is face to face with her Maker, Keeper and Lover and she is lost for words. The clear call across the ages is that of Yahweh's revelation to Moses: 'If they ask me what is his name, what am I to tell them?' And God says to Moses, "I Am who I Am".' (Ex 3) Here is the great inexpressible Presence of Annunciation, who will only be known as Mary offers her self-effacing *Fiat*. Now this same Living Presence invites us all to 'behold'.

… past my wit and my understanding, for they are the highest of all words I know. Therefore the words may not be declared here, yet everyone may receive them, coming to our Lord's meaning with love and understanding insofar as God gives them grace.

[27] THE THIRTEENTH SHOWING

Now Julian begins to examine the precise nature of sin; but at once she is faced with a conundrum. While she is acutely aware of the enormity of Adam's falling and its consequences, she finds she cannot lay a finger on its reality. Like quicksilver, it flees the finger: 'but all this while, I never once saw sin'.

Then our Lord took my mind back to the longing I had for him before. And I thought if it were not for sin, we should all have been clean and in our Lord's liking, as when he made us. But Jesus answered with these words, saying: 'Sin is behovely, but all shall be well. All shall be well; and all manner of thing shall be well.'

'Behovely' is usually translated as 'necessary'. The modern transition of the word allies to behave. But here we tread quicksand: we cannot always stay in sin. In Denys Turner's academic treatment of Julian's text, *Julian of Norwich, Theologian*, he dwells at length on this same word and its delicate meaning. Not 'necessary', he asserts, but *conveniens*, the Medieval philosopher's halfway step between contingent and necessary. This vanishing stepping stone spells out our experience of sin which collapses in true contrition. Sin is certainly a fact of human life: or is it? Sin is the opposite of the good. As white is opposed to black, the one all light, the other its absence, so sin is only known by its painful effect. If we turn from God who is our only good, we 'fall into ourselves' as Julian has it; we become estranged, wanderers without a purpose. But as we turn for home, like the Prodigal, we are received back into the welcoming arms of our Father. The pangs of hunger in a distant land are no more. Such is the black hole we name sin; a necessary evil from which good arises. But also a chimera that is also known by the pain caused as we stand apart from our Maker.

Julian rightly describes it, 'all this while, I never once saw sin'.

In this naked word 'sin' our Lord brought to mind in general everything that is not good, and the shameful despising, the utter humiliation that he bore for us in this life, and his dying and the many pains all creatures also suffer, both in spirit and in body—for we all share his humiliation, that we may follow our master Jesus until we are fully purged; that is to say until we be fully rid of our mortal flesh and of all our inward affections which are not true and good.

But all this while, I never once saw sin. ForI believe it has neither manner of substance nor part of being, and it would not even be known save for the pain it causes.

[28]

Thus I saw how Christ has compassion on us because of sin. Yet God's servants shall be shaken in sorrow and anguish and tribulation in this world, just as people shake a cloth in the wind. Our Lord rejoices in the tribulations of his servants, yet always with pity and compassion. He does this to prevent them from taking any harm from the pomp and vainglory of this wretched life. We should know that we never suffer alone but with him whom we see as our ground; also when we see his own pains and his own emptying, this so far exceeds anything we might suffer as to pass beyond our understanding.

But I stood beholding this in general with sorrow and mourning and spoke thus to our Lord: 'Ah! Good Lord, how can all be well, since such great harm has come by sin to all your creatures?'

Our Lord answered most meekly and with full lovely look. He showed me that Adam's sin was the greatest harm that was ever done or ever shall be, until the world ends. But more, he taught me that I should recognize his glorious remedy. For the work of his remaking is more pleasing to God and honours humankind's salvation more, without comparison, than any harm that ever came from Adam's sin. 'Seeing that I have made well the greatest harm, I want you to know that I shall make well all that is less.'

And so it seems that sin—that mysterious anti-matter—is brought to purpose and fitted into God's process of our 'again-making'. We seem to share Christ's own 'self-emptying' by suffering the desolation that our sin and Adam's wreak. And as we suffer this 'weal and woe', we find his peace and his joy. His peace and his joy is of his making within us—'by mercy and grace'.

[30]

Our Lord wants us to make this our business, enjoying in him, just as he enjoys us. The more plentifully we accept this joy, with reverence and meekness, the more thanks we deserve of him and the more progress we ourselves make. Thus may we come to see that it is our lot to enjoy our Lord.

[31]

It was in this way that our good Lord answered all the questions and doubts I might make, comforting me greatly with these words:

As ever, Julian finds the Trinity present and intimately active in all human history.

'I may make all things well; I can make all things well, and I shall make all things well; and you shall see for yourself that all manner of things shall be well.'

When he says 'I may', I understand it to mean the Father; and as he says 'I can', I understand the Son; and where he says 'I will', I understand the Holy Spirit; and where he says 'I shall', I understand the unity of the Trinity, three Persons and one Truth; and where he says 'you shall see for yourself', I understand the union of all humankind that shall be saved into the Blessed Trinity.

'All shall be well...' is the mantra for which Julian is famed. But let her not be framed or limited by such words. 'You shall see for yourself...' What shall we see? 'The union of all humankind that shall be saved into the Blessed Trinity.'

Once again, we have a choice: do we simply read Julian's words and enjoy their lyrical poetry, or do we take them to ourselves as our living reality. Do I know the touching of my Father in my daily making, the tender, wounding glance of his Son as my Again-Maker, the warm life-giving Love of their Spirit in my every heartbeat?

Say again. What is my faith unless I take God for real, the one, simple truth in my life. We welcome our relationships, friends, spouses, children, grandchildren: all these are our living reality. But underpinning all is the deepest living reality of the Trinity—Father giving his all to his Son, the Spirit of their rebounding Love endlessly energizing. Human words cannot encompass the true nature of our God. We may only open our heart and experience his Word, the gift of his Son, our brother who welcomes us into the mystery of his Divine relationship, Three in the Truth of One.

'You shall see for yourself.'
In these five words God wills that we be enclosed in rest and peace: so shall the thirst of Christ's spirit be quenched; for this is his spiritual thirst—the love-longing that lasts and will ever last till we see that sight on Doomsday. For we that shall be saved and shall be Christ's joy and his bliss, some are still here, some are yet to come, and so some shall be alive on that very day. This then is his thirst, a love-longing to have us all together and whole in him to be his bliss. For now we are not fully whole in him as we shall be then.

For Christ Jesus is both God and man. As regards
the Godhead, he is himself the highest bliss and was
from without beginning and shall be without end. All
this was shown most plainly in every showing but
most especially in the twelfth, where he says 'I am that
is highest'.

And as regards Christ's humanity, by virtue of the
Godhead, out of love for us and in order to bring us to
his bliss, he suffered pains and his passion and then
he died; these are the works of Christ's manhood in
which he finds his joy. This was shown in the ninth
revelation, where he says: 'This is my joy, my happiness, my endless liking, that I was able to suffer for
you.' With regard to Christ as our head, he is already
glorified and impassible; yet as regards his body in
which all we his members are knit, he is not yet fully
glorified or impassible. For the same desire and thirst
that he had upon the cross, the same he has now and
will have until that time comes when the last soul to
be saved comes up to join him in his bliss. For as truly
as there is a property in God of compassion and pity,
so truly there is in God a property of thirst and longing.
And because of the virtue of this longing in Christ, we
in turn long for him, for without it no soul would come
to heaven.

[32]

Julian resumes her deliberations on the nature of sin. It is
'no-thing' because not only has Adam's sin been righted,
but our own personal sins will all be forgiven in our 'again-
making'. This latter she sees as a continuous process in our
daily lives as we collaborate with God's working—notwithstanding that we frequently 'fall into ourselves' by turning
away from our Maker. The anomaly of sin is revealed when

we realise its pain, the pain of absence from grace, becomes the motivation for our repentance. As the Easter *Exultet* perfectly expresses it, '*O felix culpa*', 'O happy fault that gave rise to so great a Redeemer'. Christ's 'self-emptying', his immersion in the global sin of humankind, comes to a climax in his passion and death, and is prolonged as he descends into hell—where he experiences a complete shutting off from the Father. Only as he rises on the third day is his purpose achieved. In the triumph of his suffering Manhood, he has brought Mankind back in potential touch with his own Loving intimacy with the Father. Yet his task is not yet done: he invites each soul to work with him, and this takes us our lifetime.

At one time our good Lord said, 'all things shall be well'; and another time he said, 'you shall see for yourself that all manner of things shall be well'; and in these two things this soul took separate understandings.

One was this: he wishes us to know that not only does he take heed of noble things and the greatest, but he also attends to little and small, to low and simple, as much to one as to the other.

Another understanding is this: that there are evil deeds done that we know of, when such great harm is taken that it seems to us that it were impossible that they should ever come to a good end. And we look upon this with sorrow and mourning, so that we are unable to rest in the blessed contemplation of God as we ought. And the cause is that the working of our reason here and now is so blind, so low and simple that we cannot know the high, marvellous wisdom, the might and goodness of the blessed Trinity. This is his meaning when he says, 'You shall see for yourself that all manner of things shall be well', as if he had

said, 'Take heed now in faith and trust, and at the last
end you will see it truly in the fullness of joy'.

There is a deed which the blessed Trinity shall do
on the last day, as I see it, and when that deed shall be
and how it shall be done is not known to any creatures
that are beneath Christ; and so it shall be until it is
done. And why he wants us to know this is that he
wishes that we be more at ease in our soul and at peace
in his love, disregarding all tempests that might keep
us from truth but only enjoying in him.

For just as the Trinity made all things from nothing,
even so the same blessed Trinity shall make well all
that is not well.

[35]

'All shall be well', and the fullness of joy is to behold
God in everything that happens; for by the same
blessed might, wisdom and love that he made everything, to the same end our good Lord continually leads
it, and he himself shall bring it about. And the ground
of this was shown in the first revelation and more
clearly in the third where it says, 'I saw God in a point'.

Julian is wrestling with the contradiction of a God who cannot
but be Love acting to perfection—he is 'right-full'; and this is
manifest in all his loving dealings and relationship with his
damaged and fallible human family. It is rather like a caring
surgeon working alone in a field hospital where broken
bodies are continually being stretchered in. The gentle
surgeon continually bends to his task, tending the wounded
with his every practised skill and enduring energies.
As Eliot puts it in *Four Quartets, East Coker*:

> The wounded surgeon plies the steel
> That questions the distempered part

> Beneath the bleeding hands we feel
> The sharp compassion of the healer's art
> The whole earth is our hospital
> Endowed by the ruined millionaire [i.e. Adam]

All that our Lord does is right-full, and what he permits to occur is always praiseworthy. And in these two is comprehended good and evil; for all that is good our Lord does, and that which is evil he permits. I am not saying that evil is praiseworthy, but I say that our Lord God's suffering it is praiseworthy; whereby his goodness shall be known without end, together with his marvellous meekness and mildness in the workings of his mercy and grace. Rightfulness is when something is so good that it may not be better than it is; and God himself is most rightfulness and his works are rightfully done as they are ordained from without beginning by his high might, his high wisdom and his high goodness. And right as he ordained it to the best, right so he works continually and leads it to the same end; therefore he is always pleased with himself and with all his works.

The problem of pain: we can dismiss a god who despises our human condition as callous and uncaring. But Julian's Christ she sees bloodied and dying—one of us. The human condition is steeped in sin, in the inadequacy of our making: yet if we accept our lot and work with 'his leading in the working', then indeed 'all shall be well'.

Mercy is a working that comes from the goodness of God, and it shall last in its working all the while sin is suffered to pursue the rightful soul. And when sin is no more permitted to pursue, then shall the working of mercy cease. And then shall we be brought to rightfulness where we will stand without end. For it is only by his sufferance that we fall; yet in his blessed love we are kept with his might and wisdom; and by his mercy and grace we are raised to manifold more joys.

[37]

Julian begins to elaborate and explore her teaching of The Two Wills—a beastly or lower will that is prone to sin and a godly will 'in the higher part' that does only good. A tricky one this, that might lead her into heresy. The last thing she is inviting is that 'all shall be well' whatever we do. She is simply convinced of the all-powerful loving activity of God's comprehensive project for his human family. All the means for our 'bliss' are to hand, Christ's 'working of mercy and grace': it is up to us to collaborate in this working, which is that of the Trinity, 'One God, One Truth'.

God brought to mind that I would sin; yet since my liking was on beholding him, I was not ready to attend to this showing. And our Lord most mercifully remained and gave me grace to listen to him.

And at this, I was overcome with a soft fear; but our Lord responded with the words: 'I keep you full surely'. These words were spoken with more love and reassurance for my soul's keeping than I can say or ever tell. For although it was clear that I should sin, most surely was this comfort shown; so too was there the same sure promise of safekeeping for all my fellow Christians.

For in every soul that shall be saved is a godly will that never assents to sin nor ever shall. Just as there is a beastly will in the lower part that can will no good, so is there a godly will in the higher part, and this will is so good that it may never will evil but only good. And accordingly we are what he loves, and we always do his liking. Our Lord showed this by his wholeness of love in which we stand as one in his sight: yes, just this—he loves us now, while we are here, just as well as he will when we stand before his own blessed face. It is only the failing of love on our side that is the cause of all our travail.

Julian may easily be misunderstood in this passage. Let us pause to examine her experience in more detail. Firstly, this is not some conjecture of the mind, rather something she has experienced. As the seventeenth-century Christian philosopher Blaise Pascal has it: 'le coeur a ses raisons que la raison ne connait pas'. Or more fully: 'The heart has its reasons which reason does not know'. We feel it in a thousand things. It is the heart which experiences God, and not reason. This, then, is faith: God felt by the heart, not by reason. When John Freeman interviewed Carl Jung towards the end of his life, he asked him if he believed in God. 'I know, I *know*: I do not need to believe', came his urgent reply. And this 'knowing' was uttered from the heart not from the head.

Paul also confesses that he has two wills (Rm 7:14):

> The Law, as we all know, is spiritual; but I am unspiritual; I have been sold as a slave to sin. I cannot understand my own behaviour. I fail to carry out the things I want to do, and I find myself doing the very things that I hate. When I act against my own will, that means I have a self that acknowledges that the Law is good, and so the thing behaving that way is not my self but sin living in me ... In my inmost self I dearly love God's Law, but I can see that my body follows a different law that battles against the law that my reason dictates. What a wretched man I am! Who will rescue me from this

body doomed to death? Thanks be to God through
Jesus Christ our Lord!

At first, Julian is reluctant to admit to her sinful nature: is
she not beholding her God? But he has some important
reassurance which 'by mercy and grace' she receives. Still
clinging to her 'idealised image' of self, she is 'overcome
by a soft fear'. As when Peter refused the truth about
himself: 'even if I have to die with you, I will never disown
you', only to deny his Christ three times before the night
was out. But, with mercy and his grace, Julian listens; and
then learns his words of comfort, 'I keep you full surely'. By
knowing her sinful outer will, mankind's natural inclination
to sin, new life is born. For, by Christ's working, the godly
inner will holds firm. This new life comes from an inner
dialogue: as dawn breaks, the cock crows and Peter knows
his triple sin. 'Going out, he wept bitterly.'
    'I keep you full surely.'
    Any human relationship will have its 'ups and downs':
partners that never disagree stand little chance of staying
together. The whole point of love is the give and the take.
But our relationship with God is of another order. Julian
learns from her Lord 'that I never take my hands off my
works'. God is all Love and may not be otherwise: whereas
we are wayward of our very nature. Thus, God's will
towards us is steadfast: while our will is fallible as a weath-
ercock. But Christ as man holds all mankind steady in his
love for the Father. Hence the wonderful reassurance of
'these five words—I keep you full surely'. We 'fall into
ourselves' but we look up again in penitence. And as with
human relationships, the word 'sorry', truly meant and
received, binds the bond ever stronger.

[38]

God also showed that sin shall cause us no shame, but will even be accounted to our honour. For just as every sin is answered in reality by a particular pain, so for every sin that same soul is given joy by love.

Our Lord in his familiarity and for our comfort showed St John of Beverley in his fullest glory above. And with this he made it clear how as a youth of tender age he was a beloved servant of God, one who loved and feared him very much; nevertheless, God allowed him to fall, yet in his mercy he kept him from perishing and made sure that he lost no time at all. And afterward God raised him to far greater grace because of the contrition and meekness he had in his life.

John of Beverley (d. 721) was first a monk at Whitby then bishop of Hexham. His feast day was celebrated the day before Julian's crisis began. He was among the most popular saints of her day; details of the public sin to which she refers are lost to us. But we know that he was exiled to the Continent where he became a penitential solitary before returning to Beverley where he was finally buried. His tomb became a famous shrine, renowned for miracles.

CHAPTER IV

I am the ground of your beseeking...

[41]

As a solitary, Julian will have spent years growing in prayer; how intriguing, then, to hear her teaching on the subject. And at once, we are startled by her approach: 'our Lord showed me...' As a Carthusian friend puts it, 'we do not know how to pray, but there is a Spirit within who does'.

After this our Lord showed me about prayer. I saw two conditions for prayer: one is rightfulness, the other is sure trust.

For many times our trust is not complete; we are not sure whether God hears us, or so it seems, owing to our unworthiness, and we feel quite empty. How often are we barren and dry at prayer, sometimes even more so when they are done. Yet this is only our feelings and caused by our own folly, coming from weakness; I have felt as much myself.

And among all this confusion of thoughts, our Lord suddenly came to mind and showed me these words, saying:

'I am the ground of your beseeking: first it is my will that you have it, and then I make you want it: now since I make you seek, and then you do seek, how should it be that you should not have whom you seek?'

And in this first reason alone, that he is the ground, but then strengthened by the three that follow, our good Lord shows us mighty comfort, as may be seen in these very same words.

I have retained Julian's delightful word, 'beseeking', rather than using its modern usage, beseech, which would weaken the force of her meaning. *Besecke*, in Middle English, can mean to pray or beg for, to seek or search after. Prayer in Julian's experience is far more than that of mere petition; at root, her prayer is encounter, inviting the Trinity, welcoming (as did Abraham) the Presence, attending to the Indwelling. Literally seeking to *Be* and therefore be-coming. What is especially endearing is the holy woman's confession from the outset that she too finds prayer tough going much of the time. And yet her teaching is overwhelmingly encouraging—'how should it be that you should not have whom you seek?' For he is seeking us with utter intent.

Beseeking is a new, lasting will of the soul, coming from grace, by which it is oned and fastened into the will of our Lord by the sweet, silent working of the Holy Spirit. Our Lord is full of gladness and delight at our prayers; he looks out for them, for he wants them longingly. For by means of his grace they make us grow like himself in condition as we are in kind. This is his blessed will, for he says:

> Pray inwardly although you think it savours you not, for it is profitable even though you feel nothing; though you see nothing, and yes, though you think there is nothing you can do; for in dryness and barrenness, in sickness and in feebleness, all the while your prayers are most pleasing to me, although you think it savours you little or nothing. It is the same with all your living prayers in my sight.

'They make us grow like himself in condition as we are in kind.' We have already learned that by our very nature

[kind] we are rooted in our Maker; our prayer conditions us to grow into this reality. Julian goes on to speak of 'the working', our collaboration and recognition of Christ's continuing task within our soul.

As well as seeking, thanking also belongs to prayer. Thanking is a new, inner familiarity with him, full of reverence and loving fear as with all our might we bring ourselves to join the work our good Lord is stirring within us, inwardly enjoying and thanking him. Sometimes this simply overflows, and we break our silence, crying, 'Good Lord, give me mercy; blessed may you be!' And other times, the heart is dry and lacks all feeling, or else there may be a temptation from our enemy: then by good sense and grace we are driven to cry out aloud again to our Lord, recalling his blessed passion and his great goodness. And the virtue of our Lord's word turns into the soul, lifting the heart so that by his grace it enters into its true work; and so, gently enabled, it prays with true enjoyment in our Lord; then is there blissful thanking in his sight.

[42]

Julian continues to share her experience of prayer. It contains and reflects upon all she has received in her Showings: how we must persevere in spite of our sinfulness. For, as she is taught, our prayer begins and ends in our Lord.

Our Lord wishes that we understand well three things that belong to our praying. The first is by whom and how our prayer arises. By *whom* he shows when he says, 'I am the ground'; and *how* is by his goodness alone, inasmuch as he tells us, 'first it is my will'.

And the second is the manner of our praying and
its purpose; this is simply that our will be turned into
the will of our Lord, with continual joy. This he means
when he says, 'I make you seek me'. As for the third,
that we know the fruit and end of our praying, this is
none other than we be oned to our Lord in all things.

This last phrase, 'that we be oned to our Lord in all things',
I take to mean that our prayer is not confined to a specific
time given to praying, but that our relationship with 'our
Maker, Keeper and Lover' is a constant of our daily living.
It can be none other, since the Trinity permeates our every
breath and heartbeat.

This is our Lord's will, that both our praying and our
trust be equally generous. I believe we do not truly
grasp that our Lord is the ground from which all our
praying springs. He desires us to know truly that he
alone is full Being; and he wants us to take this ground
as our standing place and as our freehold.

(Middle English) 'our stede and our wonying': stede as in
homestead means our standing place, where we find
ourself. And wonying is dwelling place or our home. The
two combined implies somewhere that is both home and
permanent, our soul's freehold is literally grounded in God.
What could be more enabling! And yet she has more to
add.

One of the obstacles to our prayerful approach to God
is lack of self-esteem. We feel unworthy to count on any
personal encounter with our Maker. Julian addresses this
difficulty from the Divine perspective.

And by the gracious light of himself he wants us to
understand the following things. The first is our noble
and excellent making; the second, our precious and

dear-worthy again buying; the third, that he has made all things beneath us to serve us and how, for our love, he keeps them.

His purpose in all this is as if he were to say, 'Behold and see, I have done all this before you even pray, and now you are, and here you are praying to me.' By this he means that the greatest deeds are already accomplished, as holy Church teaches us. As we behold this with thankfulness, we ought to pray for the deed that is being done here and now; namely that he may rule us and guide us in this life and bring us to bliss. To this single end he has done all. And this is his meaning: seeing what he is doing, we should pray for it to come about ...To see his purpose, to recognise what he is doing, and to pray for that end, this gives him great praise and then we too make great strides.

Julian continues to plead one of her great themes, that of 'the working'. Christ's saving task is a continuing labour; he invites each human soul 'in the again-making' to join him in his loving deeds.

Therefore it is up to us to work diligently, and when we have done all we should do, to count it as nothing, for that is the truth. We should do as best we may, counting truly on his mercy and grace, and all that fails us we shall find in him.

And this is what he means where he says, 'I am the ground of all your seeking'. And in this blissful word that came with the showing I knew we would overcome all our weakness, all our doubtful dreads.

[43]

Julian knows that prayer is essentially simple: 'prayer witnesses to the soul's will being like to God's will'. And it

is always of his doing; it is God who prompts us to pray by
the gift of his Spirit of Love who prays in us.

Prayer makes the soul one with God; for even though
the soul is always alike to God in its nature and
substance, since it is restored by grace, yet often it is
unlike him for the sin on our part. So that prayer
witnesses to the soul's will being like to God's will;
then is our conscience healed as we are enabled by
grace.

This is how he teaches us to pray, firmly trusting
that we shall have it; for he holds us in love and wants
us to partner him in his good deed. Therefore he stirs
us in prayer to do what pleases him.

When our courteous Lord shows himself by grace
to our soul, we have all our desire; in that time we see
fit to leave aside prayer as all our attention, all our
might is set wholly on beholding him. For now our
reasons for prayer come together in the sight and
contemplation of him to whom we pray, marvellously
enjoying him with reverent dread and such great
sweetness and delight that our prayer is nothing
anymore: instead it is he that stirs within us.

Yet this prayer of contemplation is no permanent gift;
frequently we are left, as it seems, to our own devices. And
we must work at our prayer with perseverance and hope,
trusting in God's will and in his ever-loving Presence. Again,
Julian shares her experience and advice on prayer. She
speaks of making oneself *buxum to God*, that is to say
meek, gracious, obliging.

And I know very well that the more the soul sees of
God, the more it desires him by his grace. But when
we see him no longer, then we feel the need and cause
to pray—its very failing enables us to find Jesus. For

when the soul is set about and troubled and left alone in restlessness, then is the time to pray so as to make oneself supple and buxom to God. As to himself, no manner of prayer may make God supple to us since his love is ever alike in our regard.

[44]

The Christian mystic will always point to the dynamic activity of the Trinity in prayer. In some manner, and words cannot contain the truth, we witness and partake of the Father's consuming Love for his Son and the Son's whole-hearted return of that same Love who is the Spirit between them. This *perichoresis*, the dancing or interpenetration of the Three Persons, pours into the human soul—that is to say, it is always present, but we are only sometimes given partial awareness of this state.

Time and again God showed in all these revelations that we work his will always and do him honour continually without stint. And the nature of this work was shown in the first revelation in a marvellous ground, for it was shown in the working of the soul of our blissful lady Saint Mary, in all her truth and wisdom. And I hope, by the grace of God, to tell it just as I saw.

Truth sees God, and wisdom beholds God, and of these two comes the third: that is, a holy marvellous delight in God, which is Love. For where truth and wisdom truly are, there too is love flowing from them both, and all is of God's making; for he is the endless sovereign truth, endless sovereign wisdom, endless sovereign love—unmade. And the soul is a creature *in* God, that has the same properties though they be made. And so now and evermore it does what it was made for: it sees God, it beholds God and it loves God.

And because of this, God takes enjoyment in his creature, and the creature in God, both endlessly marvelling. In which marvelling we see our God, our Lord, our Maker, so high, so great and so good compared to that which is made, so that of ourselves we seem nothing.

[45]

God judges us by our human nature, which he keeps forever one with him, where it is whole and safe without end; and this judgement stems from his rightfulness. By contrast, before human beings we are judged by our changing sensuality, which seems now one thing, now another, according to which part it takes after and how it shows outwardly. And so this judgement is wayward; for sometimes it is good and tolerant, then it touches on God's rightfulness; yet when it is hard and grievous our good Lord Jesus reforms it by his mercy and grace through the merit of his blessed passion, and so it is brought into his rightfulness.

The first judgement comes from God's rightfulness, that is, of his high endless love; and this is that fair and gentle judgement that was shown in all this lovely revelation where I saw that he assigned no manner of blame to us.

I could not fully rest at ease ... due to the Church's own judgement ... by the same judgement I knew that sinners must at some time deserve blame and wrath. Yet I could see neither of these two in God.

To all of this, I had no other answer but a marvellous example of a lord and a servant ... where it was powerfully shown.

[46]

'His charity and his unity suffers him not to be wroth...' In spite of all our human weakness, the waywardness of our sensuality, God is never out of love with us. That would simply be against his very nature.

Here in our passing life we live in our sensuality so that we may never know our true self, except in faith; when we come to know and see truly, then we shall truly see and clearly know our Lord God in fullness of joy.

I saw quite plainly that our Lord was never wroth nor ever shall be, for he is God, he is life, he is truth, he is love, he is peace; while his charity and his unity suffers him not to be wroth. Our soul is oned to him, who is unchangeable goodness, and between God and our soul there is neither wrath nor need of forgiveness in his sight.

In the following three chapters, Julian continues ever more desperately to comprehend the nature of sin: why it is so unremitting and so damaging. 'God has no wrath': is he then indifferent. All this turmoil gives way to chapter 51, when the parable of the lord and the servant offers a glorious answer.

[47]

I understood that we are changeable in this life: overcome by frailty, we fall into sin. We lose all our strength, all common sense—also our will is overlaid; in these moments, we feel nothing but tempest, sorrow and woe. And the cause of all this is blindness: we cannot see God. For if we were to see continually, then there would be none of this mischief.

In spite of all this, I knew in this showing of God that such a way of seeing him cannot be continuous in this life, by reason of his own dignity and so that our endless joy may grow. And therefore we often fail in his sight, and presently we fall into ourselves.

[48]

Our failing is dreadful, our falling is shameful, our dying is sorrowful; but in all this, the sweet eye of pity and love never looks away from us, neither does the working of mercy cease. For I beheld the property of mercy, and I beheld the property of grace. And these have two ways of working in one same love.

[49]

Our Lord God, of his very nature, may not forgive since he may never be angry—for that would be impossible. Our whole life is grounded and rooted in love, for without love we may not live. And therefore once the soul, by God's special grace, sees to such a degree the high wonder of the goodness of God that we are oned to him in love without end, it is utterly impossible that God should be wroth. For wrath and friendship are two opposites. And I saw no manner of wrath in God, neither for a short nor a long time, for in truth, as I understood, if God could be wroth even for a touch, then we should have no more life, nor standing place, nor being.

It is this wrath and contrariness within us that brings us tribulation, unease and woe due to our blindness and frailty, yet we are sure and safe so that, by the merciful keeping of God, we will not perish. Thus I saw that God is our very peace, and he is our sure keeper when we are no longer at peace within ourselves. And he works continually to bring us into endless peace.

[50]

In spite of her best reasoning and notwithstanding all these reassurances, Julian has still not solved the dilemma of sin in the sight of God's unwavering love.

In this mortal life, mercy and forgiveness is the path that leads us steadily to grace. And because of the tempest and sorrow that fall across our way, we are often dead; yet in the sight of God, the soul that shall be saved was never dead nor will it be. Yet I wondered, thinking to myself:

> Good Lord, I see that you are very truth, and I well know that we sin grievously every day and are much to be blamed; and I can never avoid this truth, yet on your part, I can see no suggestion of blame. How may this be so?

I cried inwardly with all my might, seeking God's help, begging him thus: 'Ah! Lord Jesus, King of bliss, how shall I ever be saved? Who is there to teach me and tell me what I need to know, if all the while I may not see it in you?'

After this agonising prayer which echoes Paul's outburst in Romans, chapter 51 unfolds, bringing with it the first inklings of an answer, her parable of the Lord and the Servant.

Julian's triumphant vision emerges after much personal struggle to understand its full meaning. Christ has taken Adam's worn and stained smock by falling into the Maiden's womb, just as Adam first fell into 'the boggy dell' through his disobedience. By the Servant's labours, by the rending of his earthly smock, he honours his Lord in such a way that he is transformed in glory. And all this worthy labour he has gladly undertaken so that he is now 'in the highest nobility of the Father's joys'. And most importantly: 'now is the spouse, God's Son, in peace with his beloved wife who is the fair Maiden of endless joy'.

CHAPTER V

[52]

We examined the central importance of chapter 51, the Parable of the Lord and his Servant at the start. Once Julian has unravelled the lesson of her parable in this, her longest chapter, her mood changes dramatically as if an all-enveloping fog has lifted. She is free to explore the inner workings of mercy and grace that flow from Adam's fall and our own continual failings. She bursts out in lyrical song to express God's working within the human soul. Her powerful summary of her insight as to how the Trinity relates continually with us 'in the working' is voiced with simple authority: her theology cannot be faulted, her every expression is 'blissful'.

And thus it I saw that God rejoices that he is our Father, God enjoys that he is our Mother and God rejoices that he is our true Spouse and our soul his beloved wife. And Christ rejoices that he is our brother and Jesus rejoices that he is our Saviour.

These are five high joys, as I understand, in which he wills that we rejoice [with him], him praising, him thanking, him loving, him endlessly blessing. All that shall be saved have during their time of life a strange medley of both weal and woe. We have in us our Lord Jesus risen: we have in us the wretchedness of Adam's falling. In his dying we are steadfastly kept by Christ, by his grace that continually touches us and so we are raised into the sure hope of salvation. And by our falling in Adam, we are so broken in our feelings in different ways by sins and sundry pains in which we are made dark and blind so that we may scarcely find any comfort.

But in our intention, we await God, faithfully trusting him to have mercy and give us his grace; for this is his own working within us. He wants us to trust that he is with us all the while. For so he is in three ways: he is with us in heaven, true Man drawing us up into his own Person (and this was shown by his spiritual thirst); he is with us too on earth leading us on (and this was shown in the third revelation, where I saw God in a point); and he is with us within our soul endlessly dwelling, ruling and caring for us (and this was shown in the sixteenth showing, as I shall say).

[53]

Julian has wrestled for a long time, trying to comprehend the nature of sin. Her answer comes partially from her working at the meaning of her parable; she now has further insights. Our human duality, body and soul, 'sensuality' and 'substance', are the cause of our failing and our experience of 'weal and woe'. And yet this is the very same means by which we are saved and drawn ever closer to the Man who is the Risen Christ.

And I saw that it is his will that we understand how he takes it no harder when a creature that shall be saved falls than he took it when Adam fell. For our Lord God is so good, so gentle and so courteous that he may never apportion blame to those in whom he will ever be blessed and praised.

I saw and understood full surely that in every soul that shall be saved is a will that never assents to sin, nor ever shall. We have all this blessed will whole and safe in our Lord Jesus Christ. For by God's righteousness, all humankind who will one day fill heaven needs to be knit and oned to him in such a way that therein is a substance which might never, nor should ever, be parted from him. And notwithstanding this rightful knitting and this endless oneing, yet the redemption and again-buying of mankind is needful and speedful.

The Son of Man is one with all humankind, yet his 'falling into the Maiden's womb' and his suffering and death is 'needful and speedful'—necessary and decisive.

For before he made us, he loved us; and when we were made, we loved him; and this love comes of the kindly substantial goodness of the Holy Spirit, mighty by reason of the Father, wise in the mind of the wisdom of the Son. And thus the human soul is made of God and in the same point is knit to God. And thus I understand that the soul is made of nothing—that is to say, it is made but not from anything that is made.

It is like this: when God would make the body, he took the slime of the earth, that is material which is mixed and gathered of all material things, and in this way he made our body. But as to the making of our soul, he took nothing: he simply made it. And so is our made-nature rightfully oned with its Maker, who is substantial nature, unmade: that is, God. And so it is that there can, nor shall be, nothing between God and our soul. And in this endless love is our soul kept whole, as the letter of the revelations and their meaning shows.

[54]

And because of the great, endless love God has for all humankind, he makes no distinction in the love he has for the blessed soul of Christ and the least soul that shall be saved.

We ought to take great joy that God dwells in our soul, and even more joy that our soul dwells in God. Our soul is made to be God's dwelling place, and the dwelling place of the soul is God, unmade. And I saw no difference between God and our substance, but as it were all God, and yet my understanding took it that our substance is in God, that is to say, that God is God, and our substance is a creature in God.

For the almighty truth of the Trinity is our Father, for he made and keeps us in him; and the deep wisdom of the Trinity is our Mother in whom we are all enclosed; and the high goodness of the Trinity is our Lord and in him we are enclosed and he in us. We are enclosed in the Father, and we are enclosed in the Son, and we are enclosed in the Holy Spirit. And the Father is enclosed in us, and the Son is enclosed in us, and the Holy Spirit is enclosed in us: all might, all wisdom, all goodness, one God, one Lord.

[55]

Working out the meaning of her parable—doubtless over a good stretch of time—Julian is now beginning to understand the purpose as well as the cause of our dis-ease of 'weal and woe' in this earthly life.

In spite of our feelings of weal and woe, God wants us to understand and have faith that we are more truly in heaven than on earth. For our faith comes from the kind love of our soul and from the clear light of our reason and from the steadfast mind which we have from God in our first making. And at the same time that our soul is breathed into our body, when we are made sensual, then at once mercy and grace begin their workings, caring and keeping us in pity and love. In this same working, the Holy Spirit forms, in our faith, the hope that we shall come again up above to our substance, into the power of Christ, grown and ful-filled in the Holy Spirit.

We are sensual, and therefore failing, of our very nature; but then God's mercy and Christ's power and grace come into play. But we are 'more truly in heaven than on earth' because our substance is held safe and secure in the Father, our Maker. Thus Julian speaks of our two wills, one that is sensual, belonging to our created changeable nature, the other residing in our substance coming 'from our steadfast mind which we have from God (the Father) in our first making.'

And so was my understanding led by God to see in him and understand, to learn and to know of him that our soul is a made trinity, like to the unmade Trinity, known and loved from without any beginning; and in the making it is oned to the Maker, as has already been said.

We have this plainly stated in the Third Showing 'see I am God, see I do all thing, see I never lift my hand off my own works...'(chap. 11) Equally, we are assured, quite correctly, that if the Father failed to hold us in being, even for a second, we would cease to be.

And because of the worshipful oneing that was thus made by God, between the soul and the body, it follows that human nature must be restored from a double death. This restoring might never take place until the time the Second Person of the Trinity had taken the lower part of our nature, to whom the higher part was oned in the first making. And both these parts were in Christ, the higher and the lower, which is but one soul. The higher part was one in peace with God in fullest joy and bliss; the lower part, which is sensuality, suffered for the salvation of humankind.

Julian ends this chapter by referring us back to her Eighth Showing where she sees the suffering face of Christ; and she also remembers how as she lay dying, she preferred not 'to look up to heaven' but chose to keep her eyes 'on my intermediary', her suffering Saviour.

He offers us some measure of the passion that he himself suffered in his own life. We are afflicted by his own cross and so we suffer with him, as is our human lot. And his reason for suffering in this way? He wants of his goodness to make us heirs with him in his bliss. As our reward for the little pain we suffer here, we will know God himself without end.

[56]

And thus I saw most surely that we more readily come to the knowing of God than to that of our own soul; for our soul is so deeply grounded in God, and so endlessly treasured, that we may not come to know it until first we know God, which is the Maker to whom it is oned. But notwithstanding, I saw that, for the fulfilling and perfecting of our nature, we must desire wisely and truly to know our own soul, by which we are taught to seek it where it is—that is, in God.

Julian has just asserted, to our surprise and even disbelief, 'God wants us to understand and have faith that we are more truly in heaven than on earth'. Our eternal relationship with the Trinity that is to come, in fact, already is: if God is nearer to us than our own soul, then there is work to be done—right now. Living in our 'sensuality' will not do. We must assent to God's intimacy—just as Mary did—and live this precious relationship day by day.

And so by the gracious leading of the Holy Spirit we shall know them both in one; whether we are stirred to know God, or our own soul, both promptings are good and true.

God is nearer to us than our own soul; for he is the ground in whom our soul stands, and he is the mean that keeps the substance and our sensuality together, so that we shall never part. For our soul stands in God for very strength and our soul is kindly rooted in God in endless love. And therefore if we wish to know our soul and have communing and dalliance therewith, we will need to seek into our Lord God in whom it is enclosed.

Julian adds that the Sixteenth Showing will explain more precisely how it is enclosed.

As regards our substance, it may rightly be called our soul; and as regards our sensuality, it may rightly be called our soul: that is because they are both made one in God. The worshipful city that our Lord Jesus sits in is our sensuality in which he is enclosed; and our kindly substance is enclosed in Jesus sitting with the blessed soul of Christ at rest within the Godhead. And I saw full surely that it is our task to live in longing and in penance until the time that we are led so deep into God that verily and truly we know our own soul.

I saw that into this high depth we are led by our good Lord himself in the same love with which he made us, and in the same love with which he bought us by mercy and grace through the power of his passion. This means that our sensuality, by virtue of Christ's passion, be brought up into the substance.

I had, in part, a touching of God, and it is grounded in nature. That is to say, our reason is grounded in God, who is substantial nature. From this substantial nature mercy and grace spring and flow into us, working all things to fulfil our joy. These are our ground from which we have our increase and fulfilment; for in kind [human-kind or our human nature] we have our life and being, and in mercy and grace we have our increase and fulfilling.

[57]

In our substance we are full, and in our sensuality we are failing; and it is this failing which God will restore and fulfil by the working of mercy and grace which flow into us plentifully from his own eternal goodness. Thus his own eternal goodness makes mercy and grace do their work in us; and our own substantial goodness, that we have received from him, enables the mercy and grace to work in us.

Our substance, which is the higher part, is knit to God in our making. And God is knit to the lower part of substance when he took our flesh; and thus in Christ our two substances are oned. For the Trinity is comprehended in Christ in whom our lower part is grounded and rooted; and it is the lower part that the Second Person has taken, which nature was first prepared for him. For I surely saw that all the works that God has done, or ever shall do, were known to him in full and foreseen by him without beginning. He made humankind for love, and in the same love he wanted to become man.

And Christ, having knit himself to all those men and women that shall be saved, is the perfection of humankind. So is our Lady our Mother in whom we are all enclosed and of her born in Christ; for she who is mother of the Saviour is mother too of all who will be saved in our Saviour. And our Saviour is our true Mother in whom we are endlessly born yet we will never come out of him.

[58]

In this overpowering chapter, Julian sums up all that she has uncovered in her working out the fullest meaning of the parable: here is her final say on 'the working' of the Trinity with 'his fair maiden'—humankind. As far as might be possible, here is an overview of Creation and its Redemption from the Divine perspective: with God there is no time, no sequence, no process—only perfect, loving act.

God, the blissful Trinity, is everlasting Being; as surely as he is endless and without beginning, so surely was it his endless purpose to make humankind. Yet humanity's fair nature was first prepared for his own Son, the Second Person: then, when the chosen time came, by full accord of all the Trinity, he made us all at once; and in our making, he knitted us and oned us to himself. And in this bond we are kept as clean and noble as at the time of our making. And, by the power of this same precious bond, we love our Maker and like him, praise him and thank him with a joy that has no end. This, then, is the task which he works continually in every soul that shall be saved all according to this said plan of God.

This succinct summation must not stand alone: we need
further elucidation. Rather as a symphonic first statement
is announced, now it must be played with and revealed in
all its musical meaning. She is 'beholding' the Trinity working:

And so it is that in our making, God almighty is Father
of our substance; and God all wisdom is Mother of our
substance; with the love and goodness of the Holy
Spirit; which is all one God, one Lord. In the knitting
and the oneing he is our very own spouse, as we are
his beloved wife and fair maiden; with his own wife
he may never be displeased. For he says as much: 'I
am loving you, and you are loving me: and our loving
shall never be parted in two.'
   I beheld the working of all the blessed Trinity, and
in this beholding I saw and understood these three
properties; the property of fatherhood, the property of
motherhood and the property of the Lordship in one
God. In our Father almighty we have our keeping and
our bliss as regards our human substance, which is
ours by our making without beginning. And in the
Second Person, in wit and wisdom, we have our
keeping as regards our sensuality, our restoring and
our saving: for he is our Mother, Brother and Saviour.
And in our good Lord the Holy Spirit we have our
rewarding and our recompense for our living and our
labours which will far exceed anything we can desire,
owing to his marvellous courtesy and his high plenteous grace.

In this chapter 58, one of her boldest, Julian is on a theo-
logical tight-rope as she wrestles with the unsayable: how
the economy of the Trinity's outgoing Love impinges upon

our reality and our experience of that reality. I feel it imperative, therefore, to quote this chapter in its entirety.

For our whole life is in Three. In the First we have our being, and in the Second we have our increasing and in the Third we have our fulfilling. The first is kind, the second is mercy and the third is grace. In the first, I saw and understood that the high might of the Trinity is our Father; and the deep wisdom of the Trinity is our Mother; and the great love of the Trinity is our Lord: and all this we have and own in our natural kind and in the making of our substance.

And more than this, I saw that the Second Person, who is Mother of our substance, the same most dear Person is become our Mother sensual. For we are doubly of God's making: that is to say, substantial and sensual. It is our substance that is our higher part, this we have in our Father God almighty; and the Second Person of the Trinity is Mother in nature, in our substantial making, in whom we are grounded and rooted; and he is also our Mother in mercy in taking our sensuality. And so our Mother works in diverse ways for us, so that our parts are held together. For in our Mother Christ we profit and increase as in mercy he reforms and restores us, while, by the power of his passion and his death and rising, he ones us to our substance. And so our Mother works in such a merciful way with all his children, making them buxom [willing and pliant] and obedient.

And grace works alongside mercy, that is to say in two properties, as was shown; as for this working, it belongs to the Third Person, the Holy Spirit. He works by rewarding and giving: rewarding is a generous gift of truth which the Lord gives to those who have laboured; while giving is a courteous working which he freely performs by his grace, overpassing all that a creature deserves.

Thus in our Father, God almighty, we have our being; and in our Mother of mercy we have our reforming and restoring, and in him our parts are oned and we are all made perfect human beings; and by the recompense and giving in grace of the Holy Spirit we are fulfilled. And our substance is our Father, God almighty, and our substance is our Mother, God all wisdom, and our substance is our Lord the Holy Spirit, God of all goodness; yet our substance is whole in each Person of the Trinity, which is one God. While our sensuality is only in the Second Person, Christ Jesus, yet in him is the Father and the Holy Spirit. And in him and by him we are mightily taken out of hell and out of this wretchedness on earth, gloriously brought up into heaven and blissfully oned to our substance, with every increase in riches and nobility, all by the power of Christ and by the grace and working of the Holy Spirit.

'I have been reading Lady Julian of Norwich,' declares C. S. Lewis writing to his former pupil, the Benedictine mystic, Bede Griffiths. 'A dangerous book: I'm glad I didn't read it much earlier.' Could he have meant that its challenges might have changed the course of his life? There are several ways of reading Julian: the academic might ponder the profundity of her soteriology and produce a learned commentary; others will pick and choose, alighting on familiar passages about her hazelnut and the comfort that 'all shall be well'.

I suspect Lewis took fright at such declarations as 'God is nearer to us than our own soul; he is the ground in whom our soul stands'; 'Our whole life is in Three'. Such statements once imbibed and digested are seismic in their consequence: for they stand to uproot us and revise our compass and so offer a fresh sense of direction and impetus. I remember our novice master, George Walkerley, solemnly warning us on the eve of our Long Retreat, the Ignatian Exercises, 'you will never be the same again'. And he was right: emerging one month later, the least that might be said is that we had learned about prayer, its intimacy, its potency.

The same could be said of Julian: we will never be the same person, once we have weighed her words with an open heart. For her simple message is a call to surrender all past escapism from our Maker. 'Love is his meaning', she will sum up towards the work's conclusion; while throughout her writings, she herself is forever in the presence of her Maker, Keeper and Lover for 'I never take my hands off my works, nor ever shall, without end'.

Julian's words have the relentless tug of the tide. We may either follow, as did Andrew and John, or we might turn aside, muttering that we have too much business in hand to take matters further. But all the while 'Our substance we have in our Father...we are grounded and rooted in our Mother...who works in such a merciful way with all his children'.

Shall we continue?

[59]

We are reminded that unless evil had been allowed to afflict mankind, we would never have been rewarded with such promised intimacy. 'For it is the property of God to do good against evil.'

Since Jesus Christ does good against evil, he is our true mother; for we have our being of him where the ground of motherhood begins, with all the sweet keeping of love that follows endlessly. Even as rightly

God is our Father, so is God rightly our Mother; and this he showed in all, and especially in these sweet words where he says: 'I it am.' That is to say:

> I it am: the might and goodness of the Fatherhood.
> I it am: the wisdom of the Motherhood.
> I it am: the light and the grace that is all blessed Love.
> I it am: the Trinity.
> I it am: the Unity.
> I am the sovereign goodness of all manner of things.
> I am that makes you to love.
> I am that makes you to long.
> I it am: the endless fulfilling of all desires.

For then the soul is highest, noblest and most worthy when it is lowest, meekest and mildest. And from this substantial ground we have all our virtues and our sensuality by the gift of nature and by the help and quickening of mercy and grace without which we can make no progress.

Our high Father, God almighty, who is Being, he knew us and loved us from before time; and from his knowing, in his marvellous deep charity by the foreseeing endless counsel of all the blessed Trinity, he willed that the Second Person should become our Mother, our Brother, our Saviour. And from this it follows that as truly as God is our Father, so truly is God our Mother. Our Father wills, our Mother works, our good Lord the Holy Spirit confirms. And therefore it is up to us to love our God in whom we have our being, reverently thanking and praising him for our making, mightily praying to our Mother of mercy and pity, and to our Lord the Holy Spirit for help and grace. For from these Three is all our life—kind [humankind], mercy, grace.

And thus Jesus is our true Mother in kind, by our first making; and he is our true Mother in grace by his taking our kind that is made. All the fair working and all the sweet kindly office of dearworthy motherhood are appropriated to the Second Person. For in him we have this godly will whole and safe without end, both in kind and in grace, all of his own goodness that is his alone.

[60]

Julian expands the meaning of Christ's motherhood, comparing it to human parenting, caring for the child in its every need. She likens Christ's mothering love to our own experience, yet she shows how far it exceeds any human mother's love and care.

But now it is necessary to say a little more about this 'forth-spreading'; it means how we are bought again by the motherhood of mercy and grace into our natural home where first we were made by the motherhood of kind love which will never leave us.

Our kind Mother, our gracious Mother, for he would be wholly our mother in every way, he took up the ground of his work at its lowest point, in the Maiden's womb, with utter meekness. And this he showed in the first revelation—to see her in simple guise, a modest maid, just as she was when she conceived. Our high God who is sovereign wisdom of all arrayed himself in this low place, clothing himself in our poor flesh, so that he might perform the service and office of motherhood in all things.

The mother's task is nearest, readiest and most sure, for it is the most real truth. This task might never, nor could it, be done by anyone other than himself. We well know that all our mothers bear us to pain and to dying. Yet what does he do?

Our own true Mother Jesus, he who is all love, bears us to joy and endless living—blessed may he be! Thus he sustains us within himself in love and labour until the full time when he gladly suffered the sharpest throes and most grievous pains that ever were or ever shall be, and died at last.

He might not die again, yet he would never cease his working. And therefore he is compelled to feed us, for the precious love of his motherhood makes him debtor to us. The mother may suckle her children with her own milk, but our precious Mother Jesus, he may feed us with himself.

The mother may lay her child tenderly to her breast, but our tender Mother Jesus, he may lead us homely into his blessed breast by his sweet open side and show us within, in part, the Godhead and the joys of heaven, with spiritual certainty of endless bliss. This was shown in the tenth revelation: 'Lo, how I love you', as he gazed down into his side with utmost joy.

The property of true motherhood is kind love, wisdom and knowing—and it is good. Albeit our bodily birth is but little, low and simple when compared to our spiritual birth, yet it is he who does it in the creatures by whom it is done. The earthly mother lovingly understands her child and sees to its every need.

Our good Lord is our true mother in kind by the working of grace in the lower part, by love in the higher part. And he wants us to know this; for he will have all our love fastened to him. And in this I saw that all our debts that we owe, at God's bidding ['honour thy father'], for fatherhood and motherhood, and for God's own Fatherhood and Motherhood, are fulfilled by our true loving of God. And this blessed love Christ works in us.

And this was shown in all the revelations and especially in those mysterious, rich words when he says, 'I it am that you love'.

[61]

Here the human and heavenly models of motherhood are played out and compared, pressing home the reality of God's all-forgiving love.

Often when our failings and our wretchedness are shown to us, we are so sorely pained, so full of shame, that we scarcely know where to put ourselves. But then our courteous Mother wills us not to flee away, for nothing could be further from his thoughts. For now he wants us to behave just like a child; for when a child is upset or afraid, it runs straight to its mother with all its might, crying out: 'My kind mother, my gracious mother, my dearest mother, have mercy on me. I have made myself foul [literally, soiled myself] and unlike you; and I can never put it right without your help and grace.'

The blessed wound of our Saviour is open and rejoices to heal us; the sweet gracious hands of our Mother reach out ready and diligent about us. For in all this working he uses the skills of a kind nurse who cares for nothing but the salvation of her child. His task is to save us, a duty he delights to fulfil. And he would have us know it; for he wants us to love him sweetly and trust in him meekly and mightily.

And this he showed in his gracious words: 'I keep
you full surely.'

[64]

This chapter, somewhat singular in mood, stands apart
from her text. Julian, possibly labouring as she grows old,
laments 'the woe that is here [below] ...and the well-being
and bliss that is there'. She longs for an end to the travail
of life. But she is answered positively:

Before this time, I had a great longing and desire, by
God's gift, to be delivered from this world and from
this life.

To all this our courteous Lord answered by way of
comfort and patience: 'Suddenly you will be taken
from your pain, from all your sickness, from all this
disease and from all this woe. And you shall come up
above, and you shall have me as your reward, and you
will be filled full of love and bliss. Why should it seem
hard for you to suffer awhile, since that is my will and
to my honour?'

At this time, I saw a body lying on the earth, a body
that was heavy and ugly; without shape or form, it was
like a swollen lump of stinking mire. Then suddenly,
out of this body sprang a fine, fair creature, a little child
fully shaped and formed, nimble and full of life, whiter
than a lily; and quickly it glided up into heaven.

This heavy emphasis on pain, sickness and the woe of
disease suggests to me that Julian was writing this passage
when she was very old and hoping that her life might be
coming to a close. The striking image of the swollen lump
with the little tiny child quickly gliding up to heaven brings
to mind the numerous Eastern Orthodox icons depicting
the Dormition of the Virgin: Mary, surrounded by John and

other disciples, has just died while up above her Son is nursing a tiny infant, the pure Soul of his Mother. It is a tableau strangely poignant in its simply naïveté. The Mother who bore and reared her Son, stood by at his painful ending, is now reunited and seen as a lily-white babe nursed in his arms: a mirror image of Julian's vision of Christ's motherhood of humankind.

CHAPTER VI

Julian is about to reveal to us her Sixteenth and final 'Shewing ... [which] was in conclusion and confirmation of all fifteen'. Time for us to review all that she has offered us so far.

We began with her desperate situation: she lies helpless 'my body dead from the middle downwards'. She has been bold and earnest enough to ask for 'three gifts from God': she desires above all to witness the sufferings of her Christ as he hangs dying, 'to be like Mary Magdalene and others who were Christ's lovers'. At this time she is just 'thirty and a half years old', but she asks for 'a bodily sickness' as well as three further 'gifts': 'the wound of true contrition, the wound of kind compassion and the wound of wilful longing to God'.

'For three days and three nights' she lies apparently dying; and 'on the fourth night' the priest is sent for. He anoints her, shrives and housels her: as her final comfort, she receives the Body of her Lord. Now her priest presents the cross, saying, 'I have brought you the image of your Maker and Saviour: look upon him and find your comfort there'.

Such is the stark and dramatic beginning of Julian's narrative. She does not die but lingers in some kind of limbo, a physical stasis, as she experiences a succession of vivid tableaux encounters with her suffering Christ. First, there are seven distinct revelations of the Passion, each more vivid than the last. She 'beholds' the reality of God's love as he himself hangs dying before her very eyes.

I hardly believe what she relates bears any resemblance to a video show, a preview of Mel Gibson's *The Passion of Christ*. Certainly, what took place in her darkened chamber

over those few days and nights was a real experience of his
dying moments. But at once we realise that this was a
transforming experience that lasted her the rest of her life.
We speak of post-traumatic experience—a traffic accident,
a fire, a drowning, a battle encounter—that never leaves
those who witnessed these searing events. Julian's subse-
quent years were spent as an anchorite in the peaceful
shade of her little Norwich church; her cell would now
harbour these extraordinary revelations, enabling her to
engage with their inner meaning day after day as she
contemplated the overwhelming love of her Maker, her
Keeper and her undoubted Lover. So that as we ourselves
engage with her tender revelations, we too may slowly
come to realise, to re-live, all that God is working within
our heart and soul, this day and every day.

As we have seen, the intensity of our Lord's sufferings
are in a sense a distraction: 'if I could have suffered more,
I would have suffered more', he tells her. Yet it is not the
physical pain that is to be counted—closely as she notes
and attends to each flinching detail—it is the meaning of
this event: the Second Person of the Trinity, God's Son,
becomes the Son of Man. 'He falls into the Maiden's
womb', taking 'humanity's fair nature [that] was first
prepared for him'. Christ in history walked this earth. He
experienced every stage of human development and
growth, from foetus to birth, from suckling to soiling, from
crawling to walking, from boyhood to manhood. He
teaches in the Temple, is rejected by many; he feeds the
crowds that follow him, cures the sick, informs the ignorant, meets the Samaritan woman drawing her water from
the well, opens the eyes of a blind man. And finally, he is
cornered, betrayed and crushed out of this life in the
cruellest manner: shameless, blameless, he hangs naked
upon his cross, his mother below him, powerless to help.

All this Julian shares: yet what sense is to be had from such an Almighty mess?

The First Revelation explodes unrelentingly onto the page, but in reality upon Julian's attending awareness: 'Now at once I saw red blood trickling down from under the garland... I knew clearly that it was he himself who showed me, without intermediary of any kind'. But this shock has no sooner been witnessed than she is flooded by an even more overwhelming joy.

> Within this same showing, suddenly the Trinity filled my whole heart full of utmost joy ... For the Trinity is God, and God is the Trinity. The Trinity is our Maker and Keeper, the Trinity is our everlasting Lover, everlasting joy and bliss, by our Lord Jesus Christ.

By our Lord Jesus Christ: the wonderful Parable of the Lord and the Servant is yet to come, a marvellous exposition of how Christ's suffering task is efficacious to us all. But already, by the sudden juxtaposition of the bleeding head, pierced with his mocking crown and the intimate, touching understanding of the Trinity's working, Julian is aware of God's continual involvement with his Creation. 'See, I never lift my hands off my works, nor ever shall.'

Christ must suffer, and, like the Servant in her parable; he does so with a will. But his ultimate suffering is to be separated from his Father: 'Eli, Eli, lama sabachthani?' His cry of despair is sustained through death as he falls, as did Adam, into hell. But now, by the power of Love, he lifts up all who have gone before and will come after—there is, of course, no timescale in the Divine workings—and on the third day, he is risen in glory. But his work is just begun. For as Julian discerns in all her revelations, he will work his task in each and every living soul he creates.

He is our 'Again-Maker': 'for just as the Trinity made all things from nothing, even so the same blessed Trinity shall make well all that is not well.'

And the first Seven Revelations all dwell on this deep delving into the pains, the hopeless tragedy of humankind— divorced from our Maker, until such moment as he sends his Son, our Again-Maker. For Christ, in his own human body, lives out the history of every single soul—man, woman and child that ever is and shall be. He has gone before. And yet as Cleopas and Mary, his wife, discovered on that Third Day, even as they fled from the disaster of the previous Friday, a stranger fell in step with them. Like Abraham long ago, their instinct was hospitality. 'It is nearly evening and the day is almost over. And so he went to stay with them...and when they were at table, he took the bread and said the blessing; then he broke it and handed it to them. And their eyes were opened...' (Lk: 24)

[66]

We return to Julian's text, which reverts as it were to real time, that is when she is lying abed and seeming to be mortally ill. It serves as a prelude to the sixteenth and final revelation, but Julian has an important confession to impart. We might be puzzled at the anchorite's preoccu- pation with sin, not only Adam's original failing or the sins of mankind in general, but her very own sins: 'Good Lord, I well know that we sin grievously every day and are much to be blamed.'

You ask, but how can a pious lady such as Julian accuse herself in such a way; and I think the answer comes, as any striving person approaches God more and more intimately, the realisation of the gap between Maker and creature becomes more acute. We see this plainly at the moment of Mary's annunciation: Luke tells us that she was 'deeply disturbed' and later how 'he has looked upon his lowly handmaid'.

And so Julian feels compelled to tell us that she faltered even as she received her revelation, doubting they were from God. Let me offer a brief resume of this critical chapter.

At the end of an exhausting week during which she has suffered grievously while receiving powerful revelations, Julian is visited by 'a religious person', presumably a second priest. He asks after her and she replies, as if to belittle even doubt the reality of her revelations, 'I raved today!' And she adds: 'The cross that stood before my face, I thought it bled freely.' At this, her visitor falls silent and then begins to marvel at this news.

At once Julian is full of shame and feels she has sinned gravely. 'This man, who saw nothing at all, takes seriously the least word I may say.' Whereas Julian seems at that moment to have 'lost the comfort of all these blessed showings of our Lord God'. Finally, she sleeps only to be confronted by a 'fiend [who] had me by the throat; and he put his face very close to mine...there was no proper shape to his body or hands; but he held me in his paws by the throat and would have strangled me, but he could not'. This nightmare over, worse is to come. She wakes only to see smoke coming 'in through the door with a great heat and a foul stink'. She is convinced that the room is on fire and both she and her companions are about to be burned alive. She is reassured that all is well: 'And at once it all vanished away, and I was brought to great rest and peace without sickness of body or fear of conscience.'

[67] THE SIXTEENTH SHOWING

And then our Lord, opening my spiritual eye, showed
me my soul in the middle of my heart. I saw the soul
as large as if it were an endless world and as if it were
a blissful kingdom. And by the details I saw therein, I
understood it to be a glorious city.

In the middle of that city sits our Lord Jesus, God
and man, a fair person, large in stature, highest bishop,
solemnest king, most honourable Lord. And I saw him
clad solemnly, worshipfully. He sits in the soul of his
own right in peace and rest. And the Godhead rules
and cares over heaven and earth and all that there is;
sovereign might, sovereign wisdom, sovereign goodness. The place that Jesus takes in our soul, he shall
never remove from it without end—as I see it; for in
us is his homeliest home and his endless dwelling.

'In us is his homeliest home and his endless dwelling.' Julian
insists that as with the very first revelation so too with this
concluding experience 'includes a showing of the Trinity
with the Incarnation and tells of the unity between God
and the soul; with many other fair showings of endless
wisdom and love, in which all that follow are grounded and
oned'.

We are at home with the Trinity and the Trinity is at
home with us. We may not have the exact apprehension
of this singular truth as did Julian, but 'this revelation is
none other than the faith we all hold'. And again 'everything I say about myself, that also goes for all my fellow
Christians. For this is what I understood from our Lord, that
this is his meaning'.

And in this he showed the pleasure he takes in the
making of our soul. For as well as the Father might
make a creature, and as well as the Son could make a

creature, so well did the Holy Spirit will that our soul was made; and so it was done. And therefore the blessed Trinity rejoices without end in the making of our soul; for he saw from without beginning what would please him without end.

This culmination of the revelations links in to the parable of the Lord and his Servant where wrong has been righted and the relationship between the two has been restored in perfect harmony. At the same time, the entire human family is offered this same loving intimacy which is interior to the workings of the Trinity. Julian has spoken of sin as 'falling into oneself': she now reiterates our need to turn aside from worldly things so as to 'come into oneself', a reversal and negation of sin.

All prayer is encounter, a meeting with our Maker. Julian has run her course: at her beginning, she believed she was dying. Now her seeming end is a fresh start, for she has at last 'found herself', where she now *is*, her Maker is dwelling there already. She has come home, and home is where she started out.

And so I understood truly that our soul may never rest in things that are beneath it. And when it rises up above all creatures and comes into itself, even then it may not stay there merely to behold itself. But all its beholding is to be blissfully set in God who is its Maker dwelling therein. For in our soul is his true dwelling. And the highest light and the brightest shining of this city is the glorious love of our Lord, as I see it.

And what may make us rejoice in God more than to see in him that he rejoices in us, the highest of all his works? For I saw in the same showing that if the blissful Trinity might have made the human soul any better, any fairer, any nobler than it was made, he would not have been fully pleased with the making of the human soul.

And he wants our hearts to be raised mightily above the deepness of the earth and all vain sorrows and rejoice in him.

[68]

Julian is now reconciled both to her own inner self as she enjoys the 'homeliness' of God, but she is equally reassured as to the validity and reality of her showings.

This was a delightful sight and a restful showing: that it is without any end. And the beholding of this while we are here is most pleasing to God and also speeds us upon our way. And the soul who beholds it in such a way makes itself like to him whom it beholds, oneing itself to him in rest and peace by his grace.

And it was a particular joy and bliss to me that saw him sitting; for the certainty of sitting shows him dwelling endlessly. And he gave me sure knowing that it was he who had shown me all that went before. And when I had beheld this with attention, then our good Lord showed me these words, humbly, without voice or opening of lips, saying full sweetly: 'Know well, it was no raving that you saw today. But take it and believe it and keep yourself in it and comfort yourself with it and trust yourself to it; and you shall not be overcome.'

Julian sees the perfect harmony of meaning between the first revelation and this final showing as well as those that intervene.

These final words were to teach me that it was indeed our Lord Jesus who had shown me everything. And just as in the first words that our Lord showed, meaning his blissful passion: 'herewith is the fiend overcome,' so too in these last words were said in true deliberation, meaning all of us: 'you shall not be overcome'.

Once again comes the clear assurance that the revelations, their meaning and their comfort of God's immeasurable love for his creation, is no private event: they are offered to all who are willing to internalise their meaning.

And the whole of this teaching of true comfort is spoken in general to all my fellow Christians, as I have already said, and this is God's will. And these words: 'You shall not be overcome' were spoken very clearly and most mightily to mean safety and comfort against all tribulations that might come. He did not say, 'you shall not be tempted, you shall not be in travail, you shall not be distressed,' but he said, 'you shall not be overcome'.

God wants us to take heed of these words, that we may always be firm in sure hope. And he will that we love him and like him and trust mightily in him: and all shall be well. And soon afterward all was closed and I saw no more.

CHAPTER VII

This point in our narrative marks the end of a detailed account of the sixteen revelations and the meaning which crystallised from them over the years of prayerful seclusion. But Julian is not quite done. Rather like Jonah spewed out upon the shore after his awesome incarceration in the belly of the whale, Julian finds herself abruptly returned to human routine ruled only by faith. And at this very moment, she is cruelly assaulted once more by the fiend. But 'by the power of Christ's passion', which she has witnessed at length in her week of turmoil, she survives and is comforted.

[69]

After this the fiend came again with his heat and stink, and kept me full busy. The stink was so vile and so painful, frightening and hard to bear as well. Also I heard chattering, it was bodily, like two people talking; and they both talked at once as if they were holding forth in parliament [little changes over the centuries!] doing great business. But it was all soft mutterings, so I understood nothing of what they said.

And all this was driving me to despair; it seemed to me that they were scornfully imitating telling of beads [that is, reciting the rosary], gabbling them and not attending devoutly or thinking about the meaning as we owe to God in our prayers. But our Lord God gave me grace to trust in him mightily and to comfort my soul by speaking out loud just as if I were comforting someone else who was in trouble. It seemed to me that this business was unlike any daily business I knew.

We have grown accustomed to Julian's hyper-spiritual states, so that this passage fails to surprise; at the same time, it is shot through with such human warmth that verges on merriment. She resorts to a familiar ploy that was previously efficacious: she confronts her fiends with steady prayers gazing at the crucifix.

And so I set my eyes steadfastly upon the same cross which had been a comfort to me once before; I gave tongue to speak of Christ's passion, rehearsing the faith of holy Church; as for my heart, I fastened it upon God with all my trust and strength. And I thought to myself: 'You have a great business, to keep yourself in the faith, for you must not get taken by the enemy. If you were to busy yourself in this way from now onward to avoid sin, that would be a good and excellent task.' For I really thought that if I could keep safe from sin, I would be free from all the fiends of hell and the enemies of my soul. And he kept me busy in this fashion all night long until morning came, about Prime. When of a sudden they were all gone, all vanished away, leaving only their stink, which lingered awhile. And I scorned him. And so I was delivered from him by the power of Christ's passion, for that is how the fiend is overcome, as our Lord Jesus Christ has said before.

[70]

Julian is now back to normal daily life, yet grounded in faith. She muses on the reality and purpose of our lives lead by faith, by belief in the reality of God's unseen love and abiding merciful presence. She realises that faith itself manifests the grace of God's present and abiding relationship of love.

And in all this blessed showing our good Lord made me understand that the sight [of the revelations] would pass but the showing itself is kept by faith, with his own good will and grace. For he left me neither sign nor token by which to know it, yet he left me his own blessed word and understanding of its truth, bidding me firmly to believe in it. And so I do, blessed may he be! I believe it is he, our Saviour, who showed it, and that it is the faith he showed. And therefore I rejoice in believing it. And I am bound to it, to all that he meant by the following words: 'Keep yourself in it and comfort yourself with it and trust yourself to it.'

So it is that I am bound by my faith to keep it as true. For on the very day that it was shown, once the sight had faded, like a wretch I forsook it when I openly said I had raved. But then our Lord Jesus in his mercy would not let it perish, but he showed it all again to me, in my soul, more fully, and with the blessed light of his precious love, saying these words quite clearly and very gently: 'Know it well now, it was no raving that you saw today.' It was if he had said, 'Once the sight passed, you lost it and could not keep it; but know it now, that is to say, now that you see it once more.'

This was said not just for this time but also that I might set my faith upon this ground, for he adds at once, 'But take it and believe it and keep yourself in it and comfort yourself with it and trust yourself to it: you shall not be overcome'.

I am reminded of the confession of St Peter, 'You are the Christ, Son of the Living God'. And later comes his three-fold denial. The two come together to forge a fierce faith in the man who was to become the Rock and Foundation of the church. So too with all the apostles and friends of

Jesus: now they saw him in the flesh and then he was taken from them. Their lives must now be lived in the belief of his on-going love and presence.

One further example of this necessary sea-change is related by Luke. The husband and wife disciples flee back to their home in Emmaus—Mary Cleopas was one of the two Marys who stood beside Christ's Mother as he hung upon the Cross. Jesus falls in step with them as they mourn his absence: they give him the hospitality of their home— when he breaks bread to reveal himself as their abiding comfort.

Julian continues by including all her 'even Christians' in the same faithful task.

In the six words that follow, when he says 'take it', he means to fasten it faithfully in our heart, for he wills that it dwell with us in faith until our life's end, and after that in the fullness of joy, willing that we have lasting trust in his blissful promises, knowing his goodness. For our faith is opposed in various ways by our own blindness and the spiritual enemy, within and without, and therefore our precious Lover helps us with spiritual sight and true teaching on many matters, within and without, so that we may know him. And therefore in whatever way he instructs us, he wants us to discern him wisely, receive him sweetly and keep ourselves in him faithfully. For above the faith there is no goodness left in this life, as I see it; and beneath the faith there is no help to the soul, but only in the faith: that is where the Lord wills us to keep ourselves. And so we must keep ourselves in the faith by his goodness and his own working and, when he permits it, our faith is tested by the spiritual conflict so that we become strong. For if our faith has no conflict it would deserve no reward, as I understand our Lord's meaning.

[71]

The understanding of our Lord's meaning is fully taken to heart: the following chapter is one of warmest intimacy, full of hope and joy in the abiding loving presence of Christ. Julian's Middle English expression has the poetic lilt of the Jesuit poet Gerard Manley Hopkins: *for he havith us ever lifand in lovelonging.*

Glad and merry and sweet is the blissful expression of our Lord as he looks upon our souls. For, as ever we live, *he holds us continually in his love-longing,* and he wants our soul to look for him cheerfully and offer him his reward. And so I hope by his grace that he has, and will ever more so, draw our outward looking toward his inward looking and make us all at one with him and each of us with the other, in true lasting joy that is Jesus.

The founder of the Carthusians, St Bruno, writes to his friend Radulphum: 'Here [in the solitude of Calabria] is acquired that serene gaze by which the spouse [the soul] is wounded with love; that eye, pure and clean, which sees God.' This sentiment was so inviting to the early Carthusians that it was incorporated into their Statutes.

I understand this blissful regard of our Lord in three ways. The first is his look of suffering, such as he showed when he was here in this life—dying. And though this beholding is mournful and sorrowful, yet it is also glad and merry, for he is God. The second is his look of pity and ruth and compassion; and this he shows with sureness of keeping to all his lovers that need his mercy. And the third is his blissful look that shall last without end; and this was the most frequent and lasted longest.

And thus in the time of our pain and our woe, he shows us the look of his passion and his cross, helping us to bear it by his own blessed virtue. And in the time of our sinning, he looks on us with tenderness and pity and keeps us mightily, defending us against all our enemies. And these two are his most common looks in this life; mingling them with the third, that is his blissful look, in part as it will be in heaven. And this is a gracious touching and sweet enlightening of the spiritual life which confirms us in faith, hope and charity, with contrition and devotion and also contemplation and all manner of true solace and sweet comforts. The blissful look of our Lord God works all this in us by grace.

[72–79]

The following eight chapters stand apart from the text both by reason of their context, which is the nature of sin, and their tone. It would appear from the latter that they are penned during the long years our anchorite spent in her cell cottage propped against the humble church of St Julian. At times, one discerns definite signs that Julian is struggling; she is, after all, aging and presumably bearing physical pains of various kinds. But I also suggest that she is no stranger to *acidie*, that distaste for the human condition and all its burdens which was the common cross of the first monks of the Thebaide. The same desert of the spirit was aptly described by John of the Cross and St Teresa as their Dark Night of the Soul.

[72]

But now I must tell how I saw mortal sin in those creatures who will not perish for sin, but will live in the joy of God without end.

I saw that two opposites could never be together in the one place. The two that are most opposite is the highest bliss and the deepest pain. The highest bliss is to have him in clarity of endless life, him truly seeing, him sweetly feeling, all perfectly having in fullness of joy. So was the blessed face of our Lord shown in pity; and I saw in this that sin is the most opposite, so that as long as we be mixed up with any part of sin, we shall never see the blessed face of our Lord clearly. And the more horrible, the more grievous be our sin, the deeper for that time are we from this blissful sight. And therefore it seems to us many times that we were at risk of death, partly already in hell, for the sorrow and pain that sin causes us. And so we are dead for a time from true sight of our blissful life.

But in spite of all this, I saw truthfully that we are not dead in the sight of God, nor does ever he pass from us. Yet he will never have his full bliss in us until we have our full bliss in him, truly seeing his fair blissful face; for we are destined to this by our nature, the getting to it by grace. Thus I saw how sin is deadly for a short time in those blessed creatures who will have endless life.

The passage continues with a reference to St Bernard's much loved hymn, *Jesus dulcis memoria*—Jesus the very thought of thee.

And the more clearly a soul sees this blissful face by grace of loving, the more it longs to see it in its fullness. For notwithstanding that our Lord God dwells in us and is here with us, clasps us close, encloses us for tender love so that he may never leave us, *and is more near to us than tongue can tell or heart can think,* yet we may never cease from mourning and weeping nor longing until the time we can see him clearly in his blissful countenance. For in that precious, blissful sight no woe can last nor shall weal fail us.

And in this I saw reason for mirth and reason to mourn. Reason for mirth, in that our Lord our Maker is so near to us and in us and we in him, by the sureness of his keeping, of his great goodness.

The act of our creation is not something in time that occurred at our conception in our mother's womb but an on-going gift of life: 'See I am God. See I am in all thing. See I never lift my hands off my own works, nor ever shall, without end.' (The Third Showing)

Reason to mourn, in that our spiritual eye is so blind and we are so borne down by the weight of our mortal flesh and the darkness of sin that we may not see our Lord God clearly in his fair blissful face.

So that blissful sight puts an end to all manner of pain for the loving soul, filling it full of every kind of joy and bliss. And that was shown by the high, marvellous words where he said, 'I it am that is highest; I it am that is lowest; I it am that is all' (chapter 26: the Twelfth Showing).

Three ways of knowing belong to us: the first that we know our Lord God; the second that we know ourselves, what we are of him by nature and grace; and the third, that we humbly know what we ourselves are regarding our sin and feebleness. These were the three reasons why all the showing was made, as I understand it.

[73]

She treats of the dangers of giving into *acidie*, weariness of living. This experience was soon recognised by the first monks in the Egyptian desert. Not surprisingly, the repetition of their ascetic practices and lengthy prayers, their fasting, their solitude would wear down the human spirit.

Abbot Antony (250-353), the first monk, had a simple answer: refuse the temptation. 'On one occasion, when I was fasting, the cunning one came along dressed as a monk and carrying bread. He began to counsel me, saying: "get up off your knees. Cheer yourself up with this bread I have brought for you and a little water. You need a rest from all your labours. However holy you may be, you are still human after all. You should be careful you do not fall ill or some other fate overtake you." I listened carefully to this speech, but I gave no answer. I bowed my head and prayed aloud: "O Lord, do away with him as you always rid me of his presence".'

God showed me two kinds of sickness we have: one is impatience or sloth by which we bear our labour and our pains with heaviness; the other is despair or fearful doubting. He showed me sin in general, in which all sins are contained, but in detail he showed none save these two. For it is these two that trouble and tempt us the most, as our Lord showed me, so he wants us to attend to them. I speak of such men and women who for God's sake hate sin and are prepared in themselves to do God's will. Then, by our blindness of spirit and heaviness of flesh, we are most inclined to them. Hence God wills that they be known and we should refuse them like all other sins.

Of all the properties of the blissful Trinity, it is God's will that we be most sure of and take most delight in

his love; for love makes us strong and wisdom
humbles us. For just as by the courteous wisdom of
God, he forgives us our sin following our repentance,
so also he wants us to forgive our sin in respect of our
foolish dreads and these doubts that cast us down.

[74]

The gifts of the Spirit are first listed by Paul addressing the
Christians of Corinth. Cassian and John Damascene take
his teaching further by distinguishing between promptings
of the Spirit and disturbances from the devil. But it is
Ignatius in The Spiritual Exercises who refines the virtue of
'discernment of spirits'. Promptings of the Spirit, if followed through, bring us joy and peace: seductive whispers
of Satan may be persistent or arrive like a squall—their fruit
is emptiness and sorrow. All these masters insist upon
anyone wishing to progress in spiritual matters taking a
director, someone to confide in who will objectively discern
these innermost promptings.

We have noted how Margery Kempe came to Julian's
cell precisely on such business: were her agitations from
God or the evil one. And Julian's wise answer came, if such
movements lead to love, then they could only come from
the Spirit. Julian herself makes no mention of having a
spiritual director, but Norwich in her day enjoyed a wealth
of holy monks and priests. We know, again from Margery
Kempe, that Julian's reputation was broadcast, so that she
must have received a continuous number of visitors to her
cell, some merely curious others seeking her counsel.

Julian would have had her own chosen confessor with
whom she would herself have confided and received wise
advice. The Ancrene Riwle, set out two centuries before
her time, was imposed by the bishop on any woman taking
on the life of a solitary. As to the role of her confessor, it

reads: 'Every anchoress must, therefore, observe the outward rule according to the advice of her confessor, and do obediently whatever he enjoins and commands her, who knows her state and her strength. He may modify the outward rule, as prudence may direct, and as he sees that the inward may thus be best kept.'

Here is her own original take on discernment:

I understand four sorts of dread. One is dread of fright that overcomes a person suddenly through frailty. This dread is good, since it purges us just like a bodily sickness or another such pain that is not sinful; for all these sorts of pains help us when they are taken patiently. The second dread is the pain that stirs and wakes us from the sleep of sin. For a time we are unable to perceive the soft comfort of the Holy Spirit until such time as we understand what is meant by this dread of pain, fear of bodily death and of our spiritual enemies. This dread stirs us to seek comfort and mercy from God and enables us to have contrition by the blissful touching of the Holy Spirit. The third is doubtful dread, inasmuch as it draws us to despair, God will have it turned in us to love by our recognising love: that is to say, the bitterness of doubt dissolves into the sweetness of our innate love by grace. For it can never please our Lord when his servants doubt his goodness.

And the fourth is reverent dread, for there is no dread in us that pleases God more than reverent dread; which is most gentle, since the more it is had, the less is it felt for the sweetness of love.

Love and dread are brethren; and they are rooted in us by the goodness of our Maker and they shall never be taken from us without end.

'Love and dread are brethren....they shall never be taken from us.' I find this peculiarly touching: Julian has settled for her human condition, recognising that God's loving presence is not always discernible to the soul, but that her 'dreads' are simply masks of his presence and signposts that mark the way to receiving his love.

All dreads, other than reverent dread, that come to us, even though they come under the colour of holiness, are not in reality holy. And we can tell them apart in this way: the dread that makes us flee hastily from all that is not good and fall into our Lord's breast like a child to its mother's bosom, with all our will and mind, well knowing our feebleness and our great need, knowing his everlasting goodness and his blissful love, only seeking him for salvation, clinging to him in sure trust—the dread that brings all this about is kind [belonging to humankind or nature], gracious, good and true. All that is contrary to this is either wrong or it is mixed with wrong. This, then, is the remedy, to know them one from the other and to refuse the wrong. For in this life the profit we have naturally from dread, by the gracious working of the Holy Spirit, will stand in heaven before God, gentle, courteous and wholly delightful. And in this way we shall through love be homely and near God, and we shall through dread be gentle and courteous to God; both equally alike.

Therefore we are in great need to beg our Lord of his grace that we might have this reverent dread and meek love, by his gift, in our heart and in our working; for without this no one may please God.

[75]

Julian reveals her most tender self as she considers God's attitude towards humankind, the work of his hands. The longings—and she supposes them to be threefold—which God has belong also to ourselves.

I saw that God can do all that is necessary to us; and these three are what I say we most need: love, longing, pity. Pity and love keep us in time of our need, and longing for that same love draws us towards heaven. For the thirst of God is to have humankind in general unto himself, by means of this thirst he has drawn all the saints who are with him now in bliss. And in gaining more living members, he continues to draw and to drink, yet ever he thirsts and more he longs.

I saw three kinds of longing in God, all for the same end; and we have the same within us which also work to one end. The first is that he longs to teach us to know him and love him forevermore, as it is fitting and speedful. The second is that he longs to have us in his bliss, like those souls who are taken from pain to heaven. The third is to fill us full of bliss; and this will happen on the last day down to the very least. In this we will at last see clearly the reason for everything he has done.

[76]

The greatest wisdom that any creature may have is to follow the will and counsel of his highest and best Friend. Now this highest Friend is Jesus. It is his will and counsel that we should set ourselves to him, in whatsoever state we be. For whether or no we be foul or clean, we are all the same in his loving. For in good times or bad, we must never flee from him; because we are so changing within ourselves that we often fall into sin.

[77]

This section of our text stands as a guide to everyday perseverance in the spiritual way. There are elements of Julian's own struggle as she dwells on the pitfalls of *acidie* and boredom with daily practice and the 'falling into ourselves' by sin. But her advice and encouragement is truly meant for us. All the while she never counts herself as someone special, rather these revelations must be shared, as far as she may, with 'all my even Christians'. Her preoccupation with sin—both her own and that of the world at large—and its destructive effects is constantly analysed yet firmly countered by Christ's steadfast presence in his 'endless world ... blissful kingdom ... glorious city', as she puts it in her final revelation.

Our good Lord showed me the enmity of the fiend, by which I understood all that is opposed to love and to peace is from the fiend and his party. And through our feebleness and folly we must fall, yet, through the mercy and grace of the Holy Spirit, we are able to rise up again by love and meekness with even more joy. And if our enemy wins anything from our falling, for such is his liking, he loses far more when we rise up again by love and meekness. And this sorrow that he would make us turns back upon himself. That is why our Lord scorned him; and it made me laugh mightily.

This, then, is the remedy: that we be aware of our wretchedness and flee to our Lord; for the greater be our need, the more speedily must we come near him. And we could sum up our state in these words: 'I know well that I have a sharp pain, but our Lord is almighty and is able to punish me skilfully, and he is all goodness and loves me with every tenderness.'

And we need to stay awhile and behold this; for it is loving meekness in a sinful soul, brought about by mercy and grace in the Holy Spirit, when we gladly and willingly accept the scourge and chastisement that our Lord himself decides to give us. And it will be very tender and most easy, if we will only hold ourselves content with him and all that he does.

When we have mind of his own passion, with pity and love, then we suffer with him, just as his friends did when they saw it for themselves. And this was shown in the thirteenth revelation: 'Do not accuse yourself overmuch, nor imagine that all your troubles and woe are because of your trespasses; for it is not my will that you are heavy and unduly full of sorrow. Whatever you do, you will have sorrow. Therefore I want you to understand it is your penance and you will see in truth that all this life is a penance that is for your benefit.'

And this is the endless joy for us that our Lord means, that he will be our bliss when we are there, yet he is our keeper while we are here.

Flee to our Lord and we shall be comforted; let us touch him and we will be made clean; cling to him and we will be sure and safe from all manner of peril; for our courteous Lord wills that we be as homely with him as heart may think or soul desire.

But we must take care not to be so familiar that we neglect courtesy. For our Lord himself is sovereign homeliness; yet as homely as he is, so is he courteous.

Blessed may he be!

[78]

This chapter could easily arise from the advice Julian would give to the steady trickle of penitents who came to her cell for spiritual advice and encouragement. For every one who came to her door, there would have been nine walking by in denial of their daily deeds. Her advice reminds us of Christ's gentle dealing with the woman taken in adultery; he saves her from stoning and sends her home at peace with herself: 'Woman, where are they? Has no one accused you?' 'No one, sir.' 'Neither do I condemn you. Go away, and sin no more.' (Jn 8: 3-11)

Our Lord in his mercy shows us our sin and our feebleness by his own sweet gracious light; for our sin is so vile and so horrible that out of his courtesy he will not show it to us save in the light of his grace and mercy. And there are four things he wants us to know. The first is that he is our ground in whom we have all our life and our being. The second, that he keeps us mightily and mercifully all the time that we are in sin among all our enemies that fall upon us—and we are so much more in peril when we give them occasion and are ignorant of our own need. The third is how courteously he keeps us and makes it known to us when we have gone astray. The fourth is how steadfastly he abides in us, not changing his regard, for he wants only that we turn and be united to him in love just as he is to us.

And so by this grievous knowing, we come to see our sin usefully and without despair; for truly we need to see it in this way. And once we have seen it so, we shall be made ashamed of ourselves and be broken from our pride and presumption. For we need to see in truth that of ourselves we are nothing save sin and wretchedness.

CHAPTER VIII

We come to the final six chapters, Julian is summing up of the meaning of these revelations 'given to all my even Christians, as I see it'. First, she sets out 'the working': how Christ has achieved his earthly task, perfectly accomplishing his Father's will; but 'now he does the last end'—he works in each individual soul. And it is our daily task to go along with his working.

[80]

There are three things we stand upon in this life; by these three God is worshipped and we are sped, kept and saved. The first is the use of our common sense; the second is the common teaching of holy Church; the third is the inward gracious working of the Holy Spirit: and these three are of one God.

God is the ground of our kindly reason; and God, the teaching of holy Church; and God is the Holy Spirit. All are different gifts which he wants us to regard and attend to. For they work continually in us and all work us to God.

We know by faith that God alone took our kind, and none but he; and furthermore that Christ alone did all the works that belong to our salvation, and none but he. And right so, he alone now does the last end; that is to say, he dwells here within us and rules us and governs us in this life of ours to bring us to his bliss.

Then it is our task from reverence and kindness to turn in haste to our Lord and no longer leave him alone. He is here alone with us all; that is to say, only for us is he here. And all the time I am a stranger to him by sin, despair or sloth, then I let my Lord stand

alone, inasmuch as he is in me. And it goes the same
way with all us sinners. But though we act like this
many times, his goodness never suffers us to be alone;
but he is with us lastingly and excuses us tenderly and
ever shields us from blame in his sight.

[81]

Our good Lord showed himself in various manners,
both in heaven and on earth, but I saw him take no
other place but in the human soul. He showed himself
on earth in the sweet Incarnation and in his blessed
passion. And in another manner, he showed himself
on earth where I say, 'I saw God in a point'. And in
other manner, he showed himself on earth as if in
pilgrimage: that is to say, here he is with us, leading
us, and so he shall be until he has brought us all to his
bliss in heaven. He showed himself different times
reigning, as I have said before, but principally in the
human soul.

There he has taken his resting place and his fair city;
out of which worshipful seat he will never rise or
remove himself without end. Marvellous and solemn
is the place where our Lord dwells. And therefore he
wants us to listen readily to his gracious touching,
more rejoicing in his whole love than sorrowing in our
frequent falls. For it is the most honour we can pay
him of all that we might do, that we live gladly and
merrily for love of him in our penance. For he beholds
us so tenderly that he sees all our living and penance.
The natural longing we have for him is ever a lasting
penance in us; and this penance is his work in us and
mercifully he helps us to bear it.

[82]

Here I understood that the lord beholds the servant with pity and not with blame, for this passing life asks not to be lived without all blame and sin. He loves us endlessly, and we sin habitually; and he shows it to us full mildly. Then we sorrow and discreetly mourn, as we turn ourselves toward beholding his mercy, as we cleave to his love and goodness, seeing him that is our medicine and knowing that all we can do is sin. And so by the meekness we get in recognising our sin, faithfully knowing his everlasting love, thanking and praising him, we come to please him.

'I love you and you love me; and our love shall not be parted in two; and for this gain do I suffer.' And all this was showed in my spiritual understanding with the saying of these blessed words: 'I keep you full surely.'

He wants us to know this by the sweet gracious light of his kind love. And if any such lover there be on earth that is continually kept from falling, I know them not, for it was not shown to me. But this was shown: that in falling and in rising we are always preciously kept in one love. For in the beholding of God we do not fall, in the beholding of ourselves we may not stand; both these are true, as I see it. But the beholding of our Lord God is the highest truth; and so we are greatly bound to God that he will show us this high truth during our lifetime. And I understood that while we are living here, it is very helpful for us to see both these truths at once; for the higher beholding keeps us in spiritual comfort and true rejoicing in God. And the other, that is the lower beholding, keeps us in fear and makes us ashamed of ourselves.

[83]

There follows a lyrical passage delighting in the Trinitarian workings of our faith. In the darkness of our living, we are lead continually by the Light—'I it am'—until our eyes will be opened to 'God, our endless day'.

I had in part touching, sight and feeling in three properties of God, in which the strength and effect of all the revelation stands; and these were seen in every showing and most especially in the twelfth, where many times it was said, 'I it am'.

The properties are these: life, love and light. In life is marvellous homeliness; in love, there is gentle courtesy; and in light, there is endless nature. These three properties were in one goodness; unto this goodness my reason sought to be oned and cleave there with all my might. I beheld with reverent dread and marvelling highly in the sight and in the feeling of sweet accord that our reason is in God, understanding that it is the highest gift we have received and that it is grounded in our very nature.

Our faith is a light, coming in our nature from our endless day, that is, our Father, God; in which light our Mother, Christ, and our good Lord the Holy Spirit lead us in this passing life.

This light is given to us discreetly, measured to our needs in the night. This light is the cause of our life, the night is the cause of our pain and of all our woe, in which we deserve reward and thanks from God. For with mercy and grace, we wilfully know and live in our light, growing in it wisely and mightily. And when our woe ends, suddenly our eyes shall be opened, and in clearest light our sight shall be full; which light is God our Maker and the Holy Spirit in Christ Jesus our

Saviour. Thus I saw and understood that our faith is our light in our night; which light is God, our endless day.

[84]

God may not show himself plainly to us in this life; but he enlightens us with his charity so that our 'working' with him in faith brings us virtue and our 'due reward'. 'And that is a gracious gift of working in which we love God for himself and ourselves in God and all that love God, for God.'

The light is charity, and the measuring of this light to us is done for our benefit by the wisdom of God; for neither is the light so large that we may see our blissful day, nor is it hidden from us; but it is just such a light in which we may live with due reward, with deserved toil and endless worship from God. And this was seen in the sixth showing, where he said, 'I thank you for your service and your toil'.

And so charity keeps us in faith and in hope; and hope leads us in charity. And at the end all shall be charity.

I had three manners of understanding about this light, charity: the first is that charity is unmade; the second is that charity is made; the third is that charity is given. The charity that is unmade is God; the charity that is made is our soul in God; charity given is virtue. And that is a gracious gift of working in which we love God for himself and ourselves in God and all that love God, for God.

[85]

Julian is fully aware that God's shaping of our salvation so that we come to our bliss is perfectly planned. It could not

be otherwise: and one day, we will see this clearly so that
we will thank him for his generous wisdom and his over-
flowing gift of love.

And in this sight I marvelled highly; for not withstand-
ing our simple living and our blindness here, yet
endlessly our courteous Lord beholds us in this working, rejoicing. And in all things we can most please him
by believing this wisely and truly and by rejoicing with
him and in him. For as truly as we will be in the bliss
of God, praising and thanking him without end, so
also we have been truly in the foresight of our God,
loved and known in his endless purpose from without
beginning. In this unbegun love he made us, and in
the same love he keeps us and never suffers us to be
hurt so that our bliss could be the less.

And therefore when the doom and judgement is
given and we have all been brought up above, then
will we see clearly in God those secret things that are
hidden from us now. Then will none of us be stirred
to say, 'Lord, if only it had been thus, then it had been
full well'; but we shall say, all with one voice, 'Lord,
blessed may you be! For it is thus, it is well. And now
we see truly that all thing is done as it was always
ordained by you before anything was made.'

[86]

I have put enough words upon these pages: it is only right
to allow Julian the last word. No surprise that she does so
with 'blissful' ease. Her book is only just begun: it is yet to
be performed...

This book is begun by God's gift and his grace, but it
is not yet performed, as I see it. For charity pray we all
to God, with God's working, thanking, trusting, rejoic-

ing; for so our good Lord would have us pray, when he says full merrily, 'I am the ground of your beseeking'; for truly I understood our Lord's meaning; why he showed it was to have it known more than it is, and in this knowing he will give us grace to love him and to cleave to him. For he beholds his heavenly treasure on earth with such great love that he wants to give us more light and solace in heavenly joy, drawing our hearts from the sorrow and darkness we are in.

From the time it was shown, I often desired to know what was our Lord's meaning. And fifteen years and more after, I was answered in spiritual understanding, with this saying: 'Would you know your Lord's meaning in this thing? Know it well: love was his meaning. Who showed it you? Love. What did he show you? Love. Wherefore did he show it you? For love. Hold yourself therein and you shall know and learn more in the same; but you will never know nor learn another thing therein without end.'

Thus I was taught that love was our Lord's meaning. And I saw full surely in this and in all that before God made us he loved us; which love was never slaked, nor ever shall be.

And in this love he has done all his work; and in this love he has made all things profitable to us; and in this love our life is everlastingly fixed.

In our making we had beginning, but the love wherein he made us was in him from without beginning; in which love we have our beginning. And all this shall be seen in God without end; which may Jesus grant.

Amen.

Lightning Source UK Ltd.
Milton Keynes UK
UKOW050001040713

213142UK00003B/8/P